IRRESISTIBILITY

IRRESISTIBILITY
Secrets of Selling Yourself

Philippa Davies

CORONET BOOKS

Hodder & Stoughton

Copyright © 2001 by Philippa Davies

The right of Philippa Davies to be indentified as the
Author of the Work has been asserted by him in accordance
with the Copyright, Designs and Patents Act 1988.

First published in Great Britain in 2000
by Hodder and Stoughton
First published in paperback in 2001
by Hodder and Stoughton
A division of Hodder Headline

A Coronet Paperback

10 9 8 7 6 5 4 3 2 1

A CIP catalogue record for this title
is available from the British Library.

ISBN 0 340 79449 6

Printed and bound in Great Britain by
Mackays of Chatham plc, Chatham, Kent.

Hodder and Stoughton
A division of Hodder Headline
338 Euston Road
London NW1 3BH

For the utterly irresistible Owen and Evan

Acknowledgements

Thanks to Laura Brockbank and Rowena Webb at Hodder & Stoughton, and to my agent Vicki McIvor for making this project so enjoyable.

Special thanks to Maddie Fenning for her love and support to my family; and to Zena Ashmore for her work on the manuscript.

I'd like to send appreciation to my friends Monika Barnes, Jacky Barry, Maureen O'Donnell, Nia Najeeb, Irene Nathan and Christina Saunders for tehir friendship and encouragement – and to my brother Gary Thomas.

Chris Kelly made the writing of this book possible. I thank him very much for his enthusiasm, professionalism and commitment to Voiceworks. He is a great friend, too.

And, as ever, love and thanks to Dai.

Contents

1

The World of the Constant Sale

Friday 16 April

7.30 am *Grab ten mins to convince Greg we both need a break and a holiday.*

7.45 am *Decide what to wear to 6.00 pm meeting?*

9.30 am *Present to board director on projects – we want more money!*

11.00 am *Convince team that projects can be brought into deadline.*

1.00 pm *Lunch with Anna – persuade her to think again about divorce!*

2.00 pm *Meeting with major client to ask for more time.*

6.00 pm *Drink with Peter – perhaps an informal job interview?*

7.30 pm *Persuade the kids to go to bed . . .*

8.00 pm *Talk Greg into going to get a takeaway?*

Do you ever think your world involves constant selling in one form or another? I certainly do – from handling my nearest and dearest, to influencing those I work with, to campaigning for causes. And in this world, the belief and knowledge that you can sell yourself to others – which I call *Irresistibility* – is vitally important.

In today's highly competitive environments, it's just not enough to be good at something. You have to be *really* good at selling this ability to others as well, otherwise they may not spot it. While some of the methods of selling this ability may be inanimate – a web-site, c.v., or letter of recommendation – the really crucial channel is live and human: how we talk to each other. Whether informally, such as a chat to someone we meet at a party, or in a more structured setting, such as a business pitch or job interview, the crux of selling ourselves is how we talk. And that's what irresistibility is all about.

Here are some examples:

You have decided to become self-employed. You have a couple of clients who you bring with you from your previous job, but you need to get a lot more. You realise this is a new demand for you and set about preparing for it – going on courses and talking to friends who regularly acquire clients and customers. You're nervous at first, but soon see that wooing clients is something you can really relish and excel at.

You are starting out on your career. You get an interview offer from the employer of your dreams. Knowing little about how to interview and with even less experience, you swot up on the subject. The interview goes well and your career is off to a dazzling start with a very prestigious company.

You are made redundant completely out of the blue. No one realised what dire straits the company was in. You've rarely thought about moving and now you are utterly shocked to find yourself on the job market. You decide to take three months off to regroup and sort yourself out. During this time, you research markets for your skills and you research yourself. You read this book and use the content. A year later, you are very happy in a new and exciting role.

You move to a new town. You know no one. You are very keen to meet friends and also to get yourself some part-time work, while the children are in school. You set up these goals as a project, which you plan step by step, and you work on improving your social skills. Within six months, you are really feeling that you are starting to belong and you are about to start a job at the library.

You are a university professor. Funding for your department is dramatically axed. You have to go to private enterprise to try to raise funds to continue your research. Although mid-career, you've rarely had to do anything like this before. As well as preparing your case, you research thoroughly the business of pitching for funding. You get the money.

Dangling succulent cherries

Now I bet it's struck you that these are very positive examples. Often self-help authors try to motivate their readers at the beginning of their books by descriptions of dire consequences that will arise if they do not swallow the book's content in its entirety. This is, of course, motivating by threat, a tactic we examine later in the book. At the start of *our* relationship, I'd like us to get off on a positive footing. So my examples take the form of dangling succulent cherries.

In other ways, too, *Irresistibility* differs from your typical self-help book. I always like to research a subject very widely, and to present my readers with lots of different ideas to choose from. I try out these ideas in workshops, where we can take a very thorough look at how we influence one another. That experience makes the advice here very practical and also unique. During the research and writing of this book, I've been fortunate to have had plenty of opportunities working with companies like British Airways and British Telecom as well as with the general public, to test the practical effectiveness of the content.

All my best and favourite books, whether it's

Steven Covey's *Seven Principles* or Nigella Lawson's *How to Eat*, become staple works of reference and I want *Irresistibility* to become one too. I have included many different situations where it counts to be irresistible, both personal and professional. So you can use the book to learn 'how to win friends and lovers' as much as to boost your professional influence.

Finally, before I tell you more about why I wrote the book and what's in it, a note about its tone. Above all else, I think self-development should be fun. The earnest tones and wacko advice of a lot of New Age writers don't do a lot for me. My approach is robust and light-hearted – in my view, the best way to approach life generally. The ideas and tactics in here are for you to have fun with, in a laboratory made up of other people. And the aim of the book is to help you really enjoy communicating with a wide range of people, so that they find your presence completely irresistible.

Why irresistibility?

Did you know that in the last thirty years, more information has been produced than in the previous five thousand? And a third of us work at managing this information: gathering, processing, retrieving and analysing it. Two-thirds of us work in the service sector, where information is our most important product. And as you're almost certainly aware, computing, our means of handling all this information, develops at a supersonic pace. Microchips double in performance every eighteen months and the cost of computing drops thirty percent every year. Probably between the time of writing and publication of this book these estimates will be out of date. A great number of us operate in this frantic environment where survival depends on flexibility.

And for organisations, even traditionally stable and predictable ones like big banks, this means that jobs are likely to be changed and lost quickly. Employees become readily disposable. Oh dear, now *I* sound like I'm using threat as a motivator!

But this does mean that we all need to be entrepreneurial about how we work, with an eye on our external environment and the marketplace. We need to view ourselves as mini-businesses, with the emphasis on what we can sell that's transferable from one job to another. Our world requires us to be quick-change artists, deftly multi-skilling from one role to the next.

Sole security

And the only security we quick-change artists can bank on is our supply of customers, in the broadest sense of the word. Our customers are people who want what we are selling. Most of us have them: whether we work as an IT advisor in a company, selling our services to internal customers, the company employees; or as a medical specialist, a geriatrician say, who knows their area of medicine is on the up; or as an entrepreneur, who becomes self-employed and builds their business on good relations with customers and clients. For any sense of job security today, confidence in our irresistibility to customers and clients is essential.

For many of us, too, the need to sell and to recommend ourselves to others may be fairly constant. Dealing with the general public as customers or clients demands ongoing wooing, as does trading with other businesses. Most markets today are highly competitive with market share an ongoing battle. This volatile world of work also means that we may have to sell ourselves at times that are completely unexpected – when we're two months into a new job, say, and the company suddenly gets taken over and we have to reapply for a position.

It's shocking really, with irresistibility such a pressing demand for most of us, that we aren't taught at school to sell ourselves and our ideas. In my line of work, people are always telling me they wish they'd learned what I teach them earlier in their lives. They tell me they get incredibly frustrated knowing that they are good at something but can't convey it, or that they have a strong case but lack the confidence to express it, or that they'd really like to approach someone with an idea, but are too shy. Their situations exasperate them and I can understand why. They are *certain* they have something good to sell, but thoroughly *uncertain* about how to do it.

And for many of us, our upbringing won't have encouraged us to learn to sell ourselves. Our cultural background, if it's British, or Asian or Chinese or Japanese, may be one that prizes self-effacement and modesty. Those cultural values will have reached us via our families and, as we grew up, we will have been strongly discouraged from enthusing about ourselves. As a result, we may find the idea of selling ourselves rather embarrassing, and we wouldn't feel comfortable discussing it with our friends and family. We may find it difficult to work out how and where we would learn these skills.

Like you, I suspect, I often find myself coming across people trying to sell themselves or their services or products to me in a thoroughly inept way. They talk at me, or ignore my psychology or seem to be on autopilot, mouthing information with a complete lack of conviction. Something is needed to help these people.

It seemed to me that this is a really useful subject to research and write about. I felt many people could benefit from practical advice on how to sell themselves better. Without patting myself on the back too vigorously, the feedback I've had to date on my workshops has been tremendous. I know that many more people could benefit from these ideas. So I wanted to write this book for you, as a member of a wider audience.

I'm sure you realise the best way to go through life is knowing that you have made the absolute best of your skills and talents. You will want to appreciate that you have realised your potential and achieved fulfilment. *Irresistibility* will help you do just this.

A junkie confesses

My name is Philippa Davies and I'm a self-development junkie. There, I've said it, confessed it and given it public airing. And I had selfish reasons for writing this book. Self-development in any form is my passion. And writing a self-development book legitimises extensive reading of the genre. Yes, you get paid for improving yourself through reading loads of interesting ideas about the meaning of life. Fantastic good fortune.

Now I know some people would interpret this confession to mean 'Yes I'm inadequate'. These people are usually cynical as a defence, because they were hopeful once, and their hope was cruelly destroyed. They hold the view that people are fixed and there's little to be done about it. I hold a very different philosophy.

My view is that, like the world, we change

constantly, and that conscious self-development is vital at certain times in our lives. We all have periods where we have to investigate ourselves in order to be comfortable with who we are. We may need to do this in order to become free to be who we want to be. And when we arrive in that glorious state of freedom, we feel easy giving more of our attention to others. Because if we've never consciously developed ourselves, then we can never really help others to do so. We won't understand the journey they need to take.

I love the idea that we can change ourselves and reinvent ourselves – that even though we may be physically decaying in later years, we can be mentally and spiritually growing and expanding. What a wonderful idea that we can travel through life continually growing and changing. Really, it's no surprise, is it, that the most consistently popular pantomime in this country deals with the ultimate story of transformation – Cinderella?

For those of you who share my zeal, the book list at the back contains my favourite titles.

The junkie's story

I was brought up in a small town in West Wales, in a family of Baptists – you know, the slightly nutty religious sect who believe in total immersion. Fortunately, having been taught by my father to enjoy argument I managed to escape the *Gloria Alleluyas* that would have accompanied me sinking backwards into the baptism pool in the chapel. This ceremony normally happens around age eighteen and by then I was equipped to argue against it, on the principle that it was an act against my individual freedom. But Baptism gave me a strong puritanical work ethic, which comes in useful when approaching deadlines.

I went to university to Hull, as far away as possible from the judgement of the Chapel elders. I read drama there, which was a big mistake, as I had low luvvie affinity. I co-edited the university newspaper, which turned out to be much more my sort of thing. Endlessly cast in *Under Milk Wood* after leaving university in my late twenties, I went back to drama school to study voice. This was much better – we did scientific things like phonetics and guessed people's psychology from the way they sounded on tape. I was inspired to start Voiceworks, a training company specialising in communication skills.

The timing here was spot on, as it was the late 1980s, when people became obsessed with image and presentation. We did well, quickly. Journalists wrote articles about us and big businesses hired us. After a few years, I thought it might be useful to formalise my knowledge of psychology, so I did an M.Sc. in Organisational Behaviour, part-time. This obsession with continuous learning has paid off. I've accumulated an unusual list of qualifications, all of which add to my expertise in communication skills. When I worked for my first prime minister (and there aren't many people who could say that), I knew my qualifications were a significant reason why I was chosen.

Today, I divide my time between Wales and London, and I write, coach individuals occasionally, and run workshops. Like many people I struggle to balance my work and home interests – I've got two small boys and a husband, with his own demanding career in the music business.

From my own experience and from current trends, I know that the skills of *Irresistibility* are going to be increasingly vital in the future – for all of us. While more and more of us spend our working hours in solitary interaction with computers, at home, or at a 'hot desk' in the office, human nature will not change. We will remain essentially social beings, needing to be in phone or personal contact to determine whether we are compatible enough to do business together. With fewer meetings, and fewer opportunities to interact 'live', when we do get together, these occasions will take on a great importance. They will be events where experts in irresistibility will thrive.

The route to irresistibility

Irresistibility, the skills of recommending ourselves to others, is a big subject. It's a subject which has been researched extensively by social psychologists, and while some of their research is useful, some of it is best kept sealed in the psychology lab from which it originated. This book includes that useful research and it is also the distillation of everything I've learned in my twelve years of advising the great and good.

Our journey covers a lot of very interesting ground. We start by taking a good look at who it is you are making irresistible. We scrutinise your essentials – your reserves of self-esteem, and what your most important values are. And at the outset, too, we'll identify surefire Laws of Irresistibility, principles that can be used in a wide range of situations. This will give you deep insight into the tactics of persuaders like estate agents and financial services salespeople – and how to resist their pressures.

We'll move on to how to behave in an irresistible fashion. We'll look at the acting skills that create charisma. You'll learn how to make seductive eye contact, and how to create a reassuring delivery. You'll get heaps of ideas on two subjects that are vital to know about: talking about yourself with ease, and how other people make decisions about you.

But nobody gets to be utterly irresistible without encountering some rejection and difficulties on the way. So in the latter part of the book, I deal with how to handle rejection, fight fear of failure, moti-vate yourself and get to the state of fulfilment known as 'flow'. If you feel that timidity, or self-criticism, or lassitude is holding you back, then this part will be especially valuable to you.

To be completely confident about projecting irresistibility to all sorts of people, in many different situations, we need to be able to control our own emotions and also manage those of others. Chapter Eight on 'Relationship Selling' gives you lots of ideas about these fairly advanced skills. It's vital reading for those of you who want to increase your irresistibility to new and existing customers.

Just before we finish our journey, we take a look at specific situations where many of us would like to be more effective. Here you will discover loads of tactics for being:

- irresistibly argumentative
- irresistibly seductive
- irresistibly diplomatic, especially with difficult people
- irresistibly significant, your own personal PR guide, and
- irresistibly self-sufficient – all about becoming irresistibly self-employed.

We end our journey to becoming completely and utterly irresistible with the ultimate lesson – how to grow irresistibly older.

The secrets

Since I started my company, it has achieved much more than my wildest dreams could have predicted. I never ever imagined, in the small Welsh town where I grew up, that one day I would be meeting heads of state and flying off to different European capitals to advise business and political leaders.

I know I'm enormously lucky being able to spend many working hours investigating how we influence one another and how we convey irresistibility. I've learned huge amounts from the great number of people that I've worked with. To any of you reading this book, I send many thanks.

Compelling, charismatic people are often described as though there is some great mystique about their irresistibility. I know their secrets. By the end of this book, you will too. Enjoy.

2

Valuing Yourself

When you want to lure others into finding you irresistible, you've got to believe that you are valuable and special yourself. When a person exudes a sense that they care for and appreciate themselves, that is how we expect them to treat us. We expect them to care for and appreciate us, too, making dealing with them an attractive prospect. Because – in case it had escaped your notice – all of us *love* to be valued and appreciated. So in the first part of this chapter, we do something essential to building your irresistibility: we identify your strengths and work out how to build on them, to create strong self-esteem.

But in this book I want to help you become *discriminatingly* irresistible. If you end up being irresistible in situations and to people who are not good for you, then I've failed. Quite often, people end up in situations and with people who are not good for them, because they haven't done enough self-questioning about what they value and what their priorities are. Without this, they lose the ability to discriminate and end up being involved with people, ventures or careers that do not really suit them.

Stephen, who'd trained as a doctor, gave me this story:

> Everyone in our family is in medicine and when I was younger I unquestionably followed suit. When I met my partner, she was leaving medicine to go into management and it made me realise that I wanted to do the same thing. It was a very difficult decision – one that caused shock and horror in my family. We even joined a support group for medics who change career. My new role, combining clinical knowledge and a managerial role in the drugs industry, is much more suited to who I really am.

So in the second part of this chapter, we look at what's really important to you in life. When we're clear about what we're good at, and what we value, all sorts of important decisions in life become easier. It's much easier, then, to sail forth and have people falling at your feet in the presence of your deeply irresistible aura.

The 'come up on to my couch' section

Sorting out those strengths

As you may well be aware, things in the world of therapy have changed. A few years back, a person would spend years lying on their analyst's couch trying agonisingly to recall why they locked their granny in the airing cupboard for four hours when they were six and a half. Today, generally, a more active and solution-focused approach is popular. This is good news, too, for all us self-help junkies, because it is an approach that can be accessed easily through books.

So this means that rather than having some bearded analyst pass judgement on the plight of our psyche, we can be very involved in improving things for ourselves: using constructive self-talk, reasoning and practical action. The emphasis shifts from a huge amount of attention being directed at our pasts and interpreted by an 'expert', to what we can do for ourselves in the here and now.

But even so, we can't avoid looking at the past entirely. However enthusiastically we tackle the 'what can we do *now* to improve things' question, some of us may find this difficult because of our views of past actions and beliefs. We may be working against powerful autobiographies that account for our lives to date. Whether we are conscious of this or not, we all have many stories that explain how we come to be where we are today. And, sometimes, these scripts have us playing the starring role of 'martyr' or 'Joe Soap' or 'victim'. If this is the case, then becoming irresistible will seem like quite an upward struggle.

How we account for things that have happened to us in the past will greatly affect how we feel about ourselves in the present. Generally speaking, we human beings tend to account for the bad things by blaming them on external factors, and good things on internal factors. So when I fail to win any money on the lottery next weekend, it will be down to the stupid machine. When I win the lottery the subsequent weekend, it will be down to my incredible intuitive powers with numbers. More about the irrationality of optimists in Chapter Six.

But some of us *consistently* account for things that happen to us in terms of having very little control. And if you've survived several plane crashes, there might be good reason for this. Excepting this degree of trauma, if your life account has you centrally and consistently being acted upon, rather than taking the initiative yourself, you will need to change it. For you to have the confidence to project irresistibility, you need to get yourself firmly back in that driving seat. Here's how:

Strengths in your script

Draw a line that represents your life from start to the present across a page. Plot on it three big changes, or turning points in your life, which involved you taking some decisions. The big changes or turning points may not have been determined by you, but you still had to respond to them.

What strengths did you show at these points? Really indulge yourself here – don't be minimalist. You are the heroine or hero in this rerun of events and your every virtue must be catalogued. List these strengths above the line, over each of the events. Savour them aloud if you like and commit them to memory. Then add any other strengths you think haven't come up with these events and bask in them, again committing them to your memory banks.

Lavish though I am in praise of myself, when I do this exercise I still hear a nagging voice keen to point out what I perceive to be my weaknesses during these events. There's a philosophy here that can be helpful. Virtually any weakness, with a slight shift of emphasis, can be seen as a strength. So indecisiveness becomes thoroughness in decision-taking; shyness becomes sensitivity; rashness becomes dynamism. You get the picture.

There turn out to be very few weaknesses that resist this slight shift in perspective to become strengths. A few years ago the British Psychological Society conference even discovered that psychopathy could be seen as a strength. This quality appears to be possessed by a significant percentage of stockbrokers in the City of London.

With your inventory of strengths, it's worth checking your current situation. Are you using enough of them at the moment? Are there situations you could change, in order to make greater use of them?

Instantly irresistible

- Store these strengths right at the front of your mind, so they are there to give you a quick boost, whenever you need it. When something important happens to you, identify the strengths.

Self-esteem and what it is

Bridget Jones has a problem with her self-esteem. And if the sales of Helen Fielding's novel about Bridget's diary are anything to go by – over a million – then an awful lot of readers can identify with the character.

But there's definitely a problem with the word 'self-esteem'. It sounds like something tangible but, of course, it isn't. Tesco has yet to bottle and sell it on the shelves. Were they to do so, I doubt they could keep up with the demand. And that's why people often scathingly describe others as having 'self-esteem' problems. It's a defensive stance: because secretly we know we have problems sometimes, too. Yes, even self-help authors have to fight the demons of self-doubt at the start of writing a book.

Indeed, we need varying levels of self-esteem or,

perhaps more accurately, we need to occasionally question our levels of confidence and resources to cope with something. If we felt utterly confident in every situation then fear wouldn't arouse our survival instincts to cope with danger. We wouldn't learn anything because we wouldn't see the need to. We wouldn't see the need to pick up signals from our environment in new situations. Perhaps some of us would never achieve anything.

We like to achieve, because the prospect of gaining self-confidence and bolstering flagging self-esteem is a great motivator. David Maister writes books that analyse professional service firms – you know, lawyers, accountants and management consultants. In *Managing the Professional Service Firm*, he gives this revealing description:

> The typical professional is apt to describe him or herself in the following way: 'I am the type of person who gets bored easily. I hate doing repetitive sorts of work, and always like to seek out new challenges. Once I know I can do something, it tends not to satisfy me any more.' This is, of course, a somewhat self-flattering description. In my experience, however, it is an accurate one. Professionals, certainly the best among them, are constantly driven to seek out the new, the unfamiliar, the challenging. The key word here is *driven*.

People who feel the constant and repetitive (neurotic?) need to test their skills against unfamiliar problems with an uncertain probability of success are frequently insecure, with a low sense of self-worth (never expressed in public), in constant need of external tests of their merits to prove (to themselves) that they have still 'got it'.

Remind you of anyone you know? There may well be a connection between high achievement and insecurity and studying this link could be an interesting research study for someone. We can all think of people who are relentlessly driven and never satisfied with what they achieve – the Margaret Thatchers, Rupert Murdochs and Robert Maxwells of this world. If contentment figures in your priorities, though, you will want to try for goals that are challenging but realistically achievable. Fantasising about some astonishing achievement that is highly unlikely will only make you feel dissatisfied with your lot.

It's sensible to identify and acknowledge one's limitations, and if they're preventing you from getting what you want, to try and do something about them. An irresistible friend of mine once persuaded me to go on an outward bound weekend with him. I am cowardly about physical challenges and spent the entire weekend feeling desperately miserable and feigning illness. Any irresistible feelings he felt for me soon wore off. If the physical cowardice bothered me enough, I'd be much better off taking up some long-term, well-taught subject like *um* . . . wind-surfing or abseiling or advanced tarantula handling.

Efficacious you

Many of us suffer because our parents, like everyone's, were never given lessons in parenting. They gave us lots of negative messages which globally described who we were, rather than describing specific undesirable behaviour we using. We might have heard messages like 'you're an awkward little cow' rather than 'you're being really difficult about helping me with the shopping'. The psychobabble for this is negative stroking. And when you're a child, negative strokes – that is, endorsements of who you are, even if the endorsement is a negative one – are better than no strokes at all. It's a sort of 'I sin, therefore I am'. You will grow up burdened with the idea that you are essentially bad.

Undoubtedly many of us need to build up our core reserves of confidence in order to deal with the difficulties that life brings – you know, that sense of 'yes this is tough and I need to be careful, but I think I can handle it'. Research in psychology abounds with examples of how strong self-efficacy – that is, the belief in your ability to succeed – actually affects the extent to which you do succeed. And once people know of your success, of course, it shapes their expectations.

A notorious example of this happened when a group of teachers were given two groups of average-ability children. They were told that one group was of significantly higher ability. After a year, the apparently brighter group received much higher marks than the control group. The teachers had expected them to be better, and as a result they became so.

So, if you'd like some more of this thing called self-esteem, you need to unlearn those negative strokes and get in the habit of:

Stroking yourself positively

Two really important aspects of confidence-building are how we handle failure and the prospect of criticism and rejection from others. These are looked at in detail in Chapter Seven. Here are some other checks and actions I believe to be helpful:

Understand your aims

It's worth starting off by checking your trade-offs between 'what you ought to be doing' and 'what you really want to do'. Are you clear about your top priorities? Check, for instance, that you're not desperately trying to live your life as a respectable married person with 2.4 children in suburbia when what you really want to be doing is living with your gay lover in the centre of town. Or maybe you're living your life as a massive success professionally, when really you'd prefer to work less and feel better. A lot of people get this one wrong.

Be confident in your different roles

You might just want to take a few moments to survey your confidence distribution. When you spread your sources of confidence across roles and areas, you are better positioned for life's un-expecteds. Defining yourself as a pretty competent manager, a good-enough mum, an astounding tennis player and a voracious if indiscriminate reader recession-proofs you far better than if your definition of yourself is confined to that of 'best manager in the firm'. That wider brief would help divorce-proof you to an extent, as well.

Develop your independence

And while I'm on the subject, get independent. However marvellous the relationship you're involved in, it's always sensible to have your own friends, your own opinions, your own money and your own feelings. Remain self-possessed. Undoubtedly, being interdependent with others is an acknowledgement of how it is to be a member of the human race. And it's a really lovely feeling being cosily interdependent with someone with whom you have quite a lot in common, while finding the differences between you fascinating. But if you make yourself so dependent that you negate your ability to operate emotionally, financially or socially alone, then you make yourself vulnerable.

Be with people who value you

Spend your time with people who value you. You are unlikely to change people who don't. If you are involved in a relationship or situation that is damaging your self-esteem – maybe a friend who takes you for granted or a bullying boss – and you want to try and make it work, then several temporary exits can sometimes be effective. In her book, *Dangerous Men*, Arabella Melville describes how she controlled her violent partner by absenting herself every time he started to be aggressive. It's the same idea that people use to help rid themselves of addictions. Remove yourself from the environment that provokes behaviour that you're unhappy with – meetings with your junkie pals or drinking buddies – and you lessen the chance of that behaviour occurring.

Keep fit

Keep yourself physically fit – exercise produces feel-good endorphins. Get guidance on alternative remedies. I'm slightly sceptical about a lot of the claims made for them, but evening primrose oil definitely does something for me and my hormones. Even if it's just placebo effect – that I'm imagining the improvement – it's worth having something to hand that makes you feel better.

Have an eye out for potential and opportunities

If something unexpected happens – and these days a lot does – contemplate the worst that could happen and then hope for the best. Visit those memory banks and remember those specific strengths and how they have surfaced in the past.

At British Airways, I run workshops for people

who've reluctantly been made redundant. I see some very different responses to their plight. BA offer their staff considerable resources in order to help them make decisions about their future, and to prepare and practise for a round of interviews. There's a well-stocked library, individual counselling and group workshops available. Self-employment is also analysed as an option.

Some people doggedly go through this whole experience with the attitude that it's just further confirmation of the hopeless case they know themselves to be. For others, they seize this opportunity to go on a journey of self-discovery, initially bemused and then positively relishing the chance it offers. With good humour and camaraderie, they often form informal support groups to get each other through.

Here endeth the lesson on stroking yourself; next I want to discuss shyness and self-consciousness.

Stroking yourself – and others

When we feel shy and self-conscious we become preoccupied with our internal states and self-talk. Hence, the saying 'shy people are selfish'. Focussing attention on ourselves, we give ourselves those negative strokes we've spent years practising and become acutely aware of our weak points. This doesn't leave much time or energy left to stroke anybody else.

The other tendency we have is to project on to

other people the messages the nasty little inner critic gives us. We assume other people present are thinking as badly of us as we do ourselves – that other people present share our particular neuroses and use them as criteria to judge us. For instance, if I'm feeling self-conscious in a situation, my uppermost thought will be: 'They're all thinking she's Welsh, forty-one, and could lose weight.'

I'm sure the irrational nature of this has struck you. In most situations – sadly, perhaps, for my ego – people aren't giving me that degree of fulsome attention, whatever their outward appearances may suggest. And even if they should choose to be attentive, it's very unlikely they'll all be sharing my top three neuroses, and using them as criteria to judge me by.

We can change the way we stroke ourselves and, indeed, stroke others, by changing our self-talk. Rather than mentally asking the question, 'How are other people judging me?' and being pre-occupied with the *effect* we're creating, we need to remind ourselves of our *intention* in a situation. What I mean by this is to focus away from ourselves to what the task ahead requires in terms of active verbs – what do we intend to achieve? And the possibilities are considerable, because in the English language there are over a thousand verbs that describe different intentions we can perform, when we communicate with one another.

In an uncomfortable situation then, rather than me assuming that everyone is judging me along the

Welshist, ageist and fattist lines I judge myself, I will consciously tell myself that I am choosing to *reassure* people perhaps, or to *involve* them, or to *welcome* them. These intentions will govern everything about my behaviour – how I look, sound and the words that I use. And if I convey appropriate intentions to people, giving them plenty of attention, I will, of course, be psychologically stroking them, in a way that I hope they will find irresistible . . .

In my experience this idea is a very simple one, but incredibly powerful. If you clear your mind, so you focus much of your attention on your intention, you will literally always be a person who appears to know what they are doing. It minimises the risk of self-consciousness and shyness marring your communication. Your attention is not on effects or hyper-sensitive to fantasies that others may or may not be having about you – it is very clearly being directed to other people.

A health service manager, Helen, described using this method:

When my first child was born, I had what I think with hindsight was some sort of thyroid imbalance. It lasted for several months and may have been made worse by the fact that my father died unexpectedly, three months after the baby's birth. One of the ways this imbalance manifested itself was through drenching sweats, which left my face and hair wet. My back was playing up as well so I took myself off to see a chiropractor who was also a doctor. She took one look at me and suggested I made an appointment to see my GP, as she'd never seen anyone sweat so much before. This was embarrassing and alarming. To make matters worse, before I could get the appointment, I had to address all the doctors and nurses in our clinic about new ways of working.

You can probably guess what happened. Just before my presentation I went into one of my monster lathers. I became acutely aware that my audience were health professionals whose job it was to scrutinise their patients for symptoms. What would they think was wrong with me? I just had to shove this sensitivity out of my mind, and to focus entirely on what I had to do at the meeting. I consciously told myself that I was there to explain to them, to acknowledge their concerns, to reassure them that this was a consultative exercise and to flatter them that we very much wanted to collaborate with them. Through focussing entirely on my purpose, I had to distract myself from other things that were happening to me.

It must have worked, because their response was very favourable, but I wouldn't like to have to do it again. When I saw my GP, I realised just to what extent I had been feeling under par.

While it may be necessary to ignore physical symptoms for the short term, as Helen did, no combatting shyness campaign is worthwhile in the longer term. If you're not sure whether symptoms of shyness and self-consciousness are health related, go and see a doc.

Instantly irresistible

As soon as you feel the slightest shard of self-consciousness, immediately tell yourself: 'This is what I'm —ing (whatever verb is appropriate) now' and just get on with the task.

- Part of the power of this approach – reminding yourself what it is you have chosen to *do* – is that it keeps us in the present tense. You're possibly thinking what *is* she on about now? Well, very often shyness and self-consciousness relate to our past experience and/or our dread of what may happen in the future. Unless we've had quite exceptional lives, all of us have experienced feelings of shame and humiliation.

- These painful memories lurk around at the back of our minds, even if we're not conscious of them. Try writing down the most embarrassing thing that's ever happened to you, or describe it to a friend, and you'll probably notice your blood pressure rising slightly, or your breathing may quicken, or you may even experience a slight queasiness. I don't want to make you feel ill, but you get the point.

- When we're anxious about the future, we can project all this anxiety on to a situation where we expect to feel shy or self-conscious. So we think things like: 'If I don't impress everyone at that parent–teachers evening next week, that's my aspirations to be a parent–governor completely down the pan.' Or, 'If I don't wow the marketing department at the meeting next Wednesday, that's my future goal to be PA to the chairman utterly destroyed.'

- Using self-talk to remind ourselves of our actions and intentions, we keep ourselves 'in the moment'. We can run a silent tape mentally that again tells us very literally what we are doing. For example, 'I'm entering the room, I'm looking at people, I'm smiling, I'm looking to see familiar faces, I'm relaxing.'
- Incidentally, this approach can help deal with tiredness, too. Having two small children, some mornings I wake up very tired and get anxious about this. But my anxiety is usually about my ability to cope at three in the afternoon – slump time. If I keep reminding myself that at the current moment I feel OK, then this reduces the anxiety.

So there you go, perhaps there's something after all in that saying, 'Oh go on, just do it!'

Getting off planet me

You may have found that something has happened in your life to pull you up short and make you examine your history. You may have embarked on a voyage of self-discovery and sought help from friendship, therapy, counselling or books. While this period may have been turbulent and revealing, you'll have weathered it and resumed attention to the mainstream of life. But some people don't get back into the mainstream. They stay on Planet Me. A fascinating place where there are endless nooks and crannies to discover and talk about. For them,

Not for the rest of us. And an unscrupulous therapist or client can exploit their clients' desires to stay on Planet Me for many years, if they choose to.

To be irresistible in any way, we have to have moved on from Planet Me. It's about knowing what you want and being comfortable with who you are. It involves a degree of comfort with yourself that enables you to focus much of your attention on to other people, and life in general.

Any of you suspecting you may have got grounded there? Then do some charity work, take up a new interest, go and mix with people you would not normally mix with in everyday living. Get back into being a contributing member of the human race.

Instantly irresistible

- Cure self-obsession by busying up your life with lots of structured activities. Your attractiveness to others will increase.

Money and your self-esteem

I couldn't finish this section without talking about money. Money by itself is a neutral commodity, but it symbolises all sorts of different things to us, based on our values and priorities. So we don't do the lottery just for the money – we do it for the freedom, or the one-upwomanship, or the security we regard the money as having the potential to bring us. Many people think having lots of money will make them feel better about themselves. Quite understandable, when we consider how much value society puts on the stuff. John works in the City of London:

> A few years ago, I found myself thinking about money all the time and with a lot of dissatisfaction. I was already very comfortably off, but still very driven. I was working too hard and long and with too much aggression. So I took stock, and realised I was thinking that when I got 'enough' – however much that would be – I would have more freedom. What I wanted to do was work under less pressure, with fewer targets. I went into self-employed consultancy and since then I've been much happier and I'm still comfortably off.

That's OK for John, who has skills that markets value and want. The rest of us may have to make trade-offs between what we want or don't want to do, how much we want money, and market forces. Prostitution can pay well, but the self-worth costs, health risks and danger are not worth it, for most of us.

Irresistible people and things never come cheap. Jewellers often shift slow-to-move goods by upping the price dramatically. Customers wrongly connect high price with perceived value. We need to remember this when we're asking for money for our own services. Let's say you've researched market values and you place yourself towards the top end, and you get no buyers. You can then offer a discount, which people like. But if you place yourself at the bottom end, and find you've buyers but are working too hard for the money and so make a substantial rise, people won't like it.

When you're negotiating for yourself, the more you regard money as a neutral commodity, well distanced from your own self-confidence, the better. Often the people who are buying your services may not be using their own money. And if you warn people that you're expensive before making your outrageous demand, they'll often think 'I'm a person who deserves expensive' and rush to give you a cheque. So be confident about setting a price for your services, and people will take your request seriously.

Instantly irresistible

- Research market rates for whatever it is you do and pitch yourself towards the upper end, even if it's the upper end for starting off.
- You may not negotiate well, because you're uncomfortable talking about money. So practise. Discuss it with your nearest and dearest and do an 'I'll tell you about mine, if you tell me about yours' with someone in a similar line to yourself. Practise your demands out loud, so you don't have a shocked expression on your face when you stammer it out.

So that's it. On our trip round the subject of you, we've looked at strengths in your script, your self-esteem, how to handle self-consciousness, and your self-esteem and money. Reader, get up off that couch and walk.

The 'what's really important to you' section

Goals are great motivators. And we achieve goals successfully when they are wholeheartedly supported by our individual values. To my mind, a top priority in self-knowledge is that we are absolutely clear about what values we hold dearest. And in today's world this is not always easy. Our culture has changed dramatically since the middle of the twentieth century. It used to be about depth and certainty, with strong institutions like the Church and monarchy prevailing. With this came a far more rigid and conformist society. Nowadays, our culture is about superficiality and uncertainty, with the lottery and Disney holding sway. With this comes freedom and tolerance, but life decisions may no longer seem so easy to make.

We get bombarded with sensationalist and conflicting ideas about how we should or shouldn't live our lives – for example, we're child-deserters if we're working mothers or drongo housewives if we're not. As I write, the latest trend the marketeers are describing is what they call the 'Tao generation': a group of fashionable types who put spiritual and meaning-of-life values over crude materialism. Needless to say, quite a lot of the celebrities who fit this description are wealthy trust-fund babes. The rest of us may have to place slightly higher priority on making money in order to get what we want in our Tesco trolley once a week.

In the midst of all this, then, the kindest thing we can do to ourselves is to take some time to reflect on what we really value, and to remember that these values often shift as our lives and times change. Like a lot of women, I imagine, I was very ambitious and driven in my career before I had kids. Now I spend far more of my attention fretting about stuff like pollution in the environment and genetically modified foodstuffs.

Constructs and chopsticks

We can clarify what matters most by viewing human beings as researchers. Our lives constantly involve sense-making: matching our own ideas and theories of what life's about against what real life throws up at us. From what's just been said we can see that when Fred – who holds a private and very dear idea of himself as Napoleon – gets his first job after college and that job involves lots of tea-making and running errands, then Fred may run into difficulties.

Our minds are full of constructs through which

we process and make sense of what happens to us and everything around us. I like to think of this as a chopstick state of mind. It's almost as though we've all got thousands or maybe even tens of thousands of constructs inside our minds, with one idea at one end of the chopstick and its opposite at the other. Some constructs will be common to all of us, but assume different levels of importance: same/different; right/wrong (unless we're psychopathic); superior/inferior, male/female, for example. How we interpret life and what we aspire to will be determined by the framework our constructs form for us.

Many of our constructs will have been absorbed in childhood. We may not be conscious of them; they may be very powerful and very difficult to realise. If life's events challenge constructs that are very dear to us, we may find them difficult to handle. Take Jane, for example.

Jane holds dear a construct that 'Good girls get rewarded/bad girls don't'. (This doesn't happen in the real world.) Consequently, when she marries, she is an exemplary wife and is distraught to find, just after having had her second baby, that her partner John intends to leave her for another woman. To endure this and move on from it, Jane will need to recognise that this construct was flawed and fallible. She'll need to relegate it to lower significance in her mind, and replace it with a more realistic construct like: 'Life needs to be a bit more about getting what I want out of it.'

Unfortunately what often happens in this situation is that we rush to generalise from the specific and create an 'all men are blackguards' construct, which can prevent us getting what we might really want – a more equal relationship.

Lots of conflicts occur because we are not clear about what constructs are most important to us. You could be a woman with a successful career who views herself through a strong achievement/failure construct. Another construct that affects your view of yourself is motherhood/lack of fulfilment. When you decide to become a mother, you will need to have resolved for yourself which construct will take top priority at that time, or you will feel very fraught and torn.

Another clash will occur with a man who has a strong relationship/loneliness construct and also a tough manager/wimpy manager construct, both of which are important to him. When he has to make decisions about who to make redundant in his department, he will need to be clear about which construct is dominant.

When you know what constructs are your top priorities then it is much easier to jiggle them around for the flexibility we need today. You may be fortunate enough to be very clear about the constructs that are important to you in different situations. If so, that's great. If you're not so clear, then you will find the following exercises helpful:

People spotting

When you do this analysis it's important not to worry about how articulate you are. As long as you know what you mean, that's OK. Nobody is marking this. It's also important not to try to be a nice person. Nobody is going to analyse your answers in order to get some insights into your dark and murky psyche. Be as honest as you like; that way you'll get most out of the process.

Choose three friends or people you work with. What's the top quality you like in each one of them? You could find it helpful to jot these down on a piece of paper as one end of a construct about each person. Then identify what you think of as the opposite quality. Here you already have some values that are important to you in judging people. And, surprise, surprise, these values that are important to you in judging others are very likely to be qualities that you value in yourself.

Then decide on the person that you like best of all. Why is that person different from the other two? And why is that quality important to you? What's the opposite of that quality for you? Your ideas are probably getting a little more abstract now and harder to articulate. But being concise is not important here. What matters is that you choose words that really describe how you feel. You are describing higher, more abstract values now.

You can do this sort of analysis on all sorts of

things: events, inanimate objects, choices of car, food and even hobbies.

A sense of achievement

I think it's useful to be clear about what it is we value when we achieve things. Repeating the above process, take three achievements and, one by one, ask yourself 'What did this achievement represent?' And again, describe the opposite. People often describe constructs like: sense of personal achievement/sense of failure; influencing others/being disconnected; nurturing/self-centredness; money/poverty; beating others/losing; others admiring me/others ignoring me; brilliant organisation/chaos; being in a group of winners/just being ordinary; creativity/dullness, etc.

Once more, pick your top achievement and ask yourself why that achievement is distinctive from the other two and what value it represents to you. What makes it especially significant?

It seems to me to be *really important* to be clear about what we value about achievement. I sometimes train lawyers in their client-handling skills. There are very clear differences between individuals in their motivation to become partners in the firm. Some will be motivated by the salary, others by the general kudos and opportunities to influence on the golf course, and others will see the role as an endorsement by their peers of their specialist expertise. When we understand exactly what achievement means to us as individuals, we are far better placed to work out what values we hold dear, and what constructs motivate us.

Your life choices

You might also find it helpful to clarify your values about how you live. Take three choices you've made relatively recently about this: it could be to do with where you live, what you do in your spare time, a career decision, food you choose to eat, a new enthusiasm or passion, or something you've decided to spend money on. Again, what does each of these choices represent to you and how would you describe the opposite? Then take the most important choice and ask yourself why this choice is so much more important than the other two. What does this represent and what does it signify in terms of what you value about how you choose to live?

Instantly irresistible

- At different times in our lives, different priorities will dominate. For many people relationships and achievement may wrestle to be top priorities when they are in their twenties and thirties, and then life choices may start to matter much more. By no means does everyone fit this norm, though. Of these three, which dominates your concern at the moment? Can you see this changing in the future? Use these answers to further clarify that you are happy with the direction your life is taking, and increase your irresistibility.

Phew! After all that analysis some of you will be glad to hear I'm going to let you get down from the couch soon. There's just one more idea I'd like to bring to your attention before we do that.

In and out people

One of the important differences between people that psychologists are fond of describing is the extent to which we are introvert or extrovert. These differences are probably determined by our brains – extroverts having more activity in the limbic system, the part of the brain that generates emotion. If you want to become irresistible, it's really useful to identify whether you are introvert or extrovert, because it can help you play to your natural strengths, rather than trying to be someone who your family and society say you should be.

In the abstract, these differences determine whether external or internal reality is more real to us. So for those of us who are extrovert, our most important filter will be the one that experiences who we are as members of groups, of relating to and being connected to others. Our focus will tend to be external and we will regard ourselves as 'people people'. We will explain our achievements with reference to other people.

For those of us who are introvert, our most important filter will be the one that experiences us as individuals, gaining clarity, meaning and achievement inside our heads. Our focus will be internal and we will regard ourselves as 'achievement-orientated' people. We will explain our relationships with the emphasis on clarity and structure.

But enough theory, I hear you shout. What does this mean in real life? I work with a very good friend of mine called Chris, with whom I like to think I have a great deal in common. But Chris is more extrovert than I am. As a consequence, he is very comfortable meeting new clients, socialising in business and forming relationships very quickly with people. He does this with great ease and with no apparent need for structure. I cope with these situations by seeking a structure or inventing one if I can't see one. But while Chris will happily chat away and make great small talk, I will sometimes blurt out 'Shall we talk about our purpose in this meeting?' Occasionally, at this point, I have caught the extrovert on the receiving end with an aghast expression on their face.

When we run workshops together, we try and play to our different strengths. Chris is freer in his approach than I am, because his focus is on how people are receiving the content, how they are enjoying the processes and how they are reacting to him. If a section is going especially well, he will throw structural constraints to time aside. Sometimes this worries me, because it seems to threaten the structure – the thing that I value above all else in holding the whole thing together.

If we're feeling vulnerable, we will tend to worry about slightly different things. Chris will think individuals don't like him and that he isn't getting the reaction he expected; I will be very concerned that I'm not getting through to people, that the content is not clear, that the goals of the workshop are not going to be achieved.

Chris excels as a people person, and even during his leisure time he will join group exercise classes that endorse his connection with others. Confession time here; when I've time to recharge my batteries I love to do it in virulently anti-social ways – through reading, going shopping (alone) or even going to a café (alone). In case it's not occurred to any of you introverts out there, writing a book is a socially acceptable way of realising your inclinations.

The irony is that we often become very good at the things that continue to concern us most. So we introverts can't have an idea without imposing structure on it . . . instantaneously. And in any difficult situation extroverts will immediately and very successfully pull out all the charm stops, while worrying still that people don't appreciate them.

In everyday conversation, people often talk

about 'extrovert' as though it's a desirable quality and 'introvert' as a rather dubious and unhealthy quality. I suspect these interpretations come from American culture, where too much introspection is regarded with suspicion. Important, too, I think to realise that these are not exclusive black and white descriptions that we could use in terms of consistently predicting behaviour. We can't really say: 'Extroverts always do . . .' and 'Introverts always do . . .'

We find shy extroverts – like Princess Diana – obviously at her most comfortable creating relationships with the disadvantaged and vulnerable. In contrast, Margaret Thatcher was a socially skilled introvert – a definite 'what-have-I-achieved-today person' who developed skills like public speaking in order to achieve her goals.

In personal relationships, people are usually attracted to someone from the opposing preference. Bill Clinton is quite clearly an extrovert (and how) and Hillary the introvert. Tony Blair, prime minister in the UK at the time of writing, is an introvert (extremely focussed), and his wife Cherie, with apparently excellent rapport skills, an extrovert.

Are you an innie or an outie?

A few days after my first child was born, the midwife came in to examine him and after a few moments proclaimed: 'Oh good, he's an innie.' Concerned that I'd somehow missed some common typology of baby categorisation, I ventured to ask her what exactly she meant. She was, of course, talking about his newly revealed belly button. Innies being, she explained, her special preference.

The whole conversation had a slightly surreal quality and it often springs to mind when I think about these preferences. So here's your opportunity to decide – belly buttons notwithstanding – whether you're a psychological innie or outie:

- If you really had to choose between the two, what would be the most important to you?
  a) Being liked by your work colleagues
  b) Being respected by them

- What energises you most frequently?
  a) Socialising within a largish group
  b) Some quiet time to reflect and mentally order your ideas

- Would you prefer
  a) A large circle of friends and acquaintances
  b) A small number of close friends

- What characterises the way you dress?
  a) Friendliness and approachability
  b) Simplicity and order

- What fills you with most dread?
  a) A weekend alone
  b) Three parties in a week where you were expected to make small talk with groups of a dozen or more

Irresistibly an innie or an outie

Having decided where your preferences lie, note that your innie skills will include clear thinking, structuring, setting and achieving goals, making order out of chaos. Where you may need to get a bit more comfortable is in those people-skills, such as making small talk and relating to people on a fairly superficial level. Get a bit more comfortable with those and you will make yourself irresistible to the maximum number of people.

Your outie skills will include stimulating others and enjoying being stimulated by them, charming people and responding warmly and spontaneously to other people's emotional needs. You could possibly benefit from getting a bit more comfortable with those innie activities of internal deliberation, mentally ordering and clarifying, and planning how to achieve goals. With this balance, you will make yourself even more irresistible.

Instantly irresistible

- Remember that we are always attracted to the opposing preference. Now you know what that involves, keep an eye out for those qualities in potential partners. Remember they may fascinate but also mystify you – a good recipe for long-term interest.
- And, finally, just to remind you: you are unique, whether you want to be or not. Everything about

you is unique, unless you are an identical twin. Your voice, your fingerprints, your genetic make-up, the culmination of your life's events so far and the interpretation you've made of these events. And unique, when projected skilfully, equals irresistible.

3

The Laws of Irresistibility

I don't know if you're like me, but I love being sold things well. Good selling is both art and science: art, in that one's feelings and deepest longings are appealed to; science, in that clear psychological principles about how we perceive and interpret can be used with reliable consistency to make us buy. It is these clear psychological principles that we will investigate in this chapter. We will look at exactly what these principles are, how they operate in everyday life, and how we can use them to maximise our irresistibility.

The laws described in this chapter are especially useful to know about and use in certain contexts. They are invaluable if you want to make yourself irresistible to employers, and also if you are selling products or services. They are essential to know about if you are in any way engaged in influencing people to act or think in a certain way. These guidelines are core secrets of influence and persuasion.

This chapter should go some way towards

explaining why we are sometimes sold ideas and things that we do not really want. For instance, I often find myself between meetings in Oxford Street, in the West End of London. If I've time to kill I'll often end up in the cosmetics hall of one of the several department stores there. Now the good thing about my job is that it legitimises indulging in all sorts of experiences for 'research's sake'. So I often find myself approaching a cosmetics salesperson in order to 'research their selling technique' (as I delude myself). As a result of this research process, I have a drawerfull at home of unsuitable shades of orange lipstick, which I've never worn.

Now you're possibly thinking 'what a sucker', but at least these experiences have given me proof of these principles in action. In this chapter, we'll look at how the principles operate in selling cosmetics, houses, clothes and even political candidates. We'll rumble some of the techniques those dubious individuals called financial services advisers apply.

Knowing about these techniques, both for our own direct usage and in order to protect ourselves, seems especially relevant today. The world in which many of us live is an extremely fast and stimulating one. We are bombarded with approaches from what Robert Cialdini in his book *Influence: The Psychology of Persuasion* likes to call 'compliance practitioners'. Clever compliance practitioners, selling us anything from soap to Scientology, know that the faster the world moves, the more short cuts we take in our decision-making. When we under-stand these laws and their application, it helps us resist pressurising tactics of which we may not previously have been aware.

The Laws of Irresistibility

By the end of this chapter you will be familiar with these magical laws: the law of reciprocity, the law of comparison, the law of consistency, the law of social proof, the law of scarcity, the law of liking and the law of authority.

1. The law of reciprocity

This law says that if we are given something by someone, we then feel obligated to return the favour. This may not necessarily be something tangible – it could be a word in an influential person's ear on our behalf, a piece of advice, a meeting with someone important who gives us their valuable airtime. The law arises from the idea that for human beings to live harmoniously together, we have to operate from the understanding that we are dependent on one another, and that we have a network of obligation. Most of us are not terribly comfortable feeling oblig-ated to others – there is a gap between what's expected of us and our actions – and we will act sooner rather than later to close that gap.

Now in the old days, when men had far greater economic power than women, this law often governed mating between the sexes. Men would buy women meals, and then expect to receive sexual favours in return. I expect it still goes on in some places. Moving on from eating and copulating, another extremely enjoyable human activity – gossip – is based entirely on the law of reciprocity. This is almost, to my mind, as thrilling a non-physical activity as the idea of: 'I'll show you mine, if you show me yours.'

Cosmetics companies and other businesses use this law through the idea of the free gift. You are given some samples of an expensive skin cream made by, say, Clarins. They have done you a favour, and so you are far more likely to splash out on the full-size wrinkle-attacker in return. This law is being practised when we are given expensive-looking brochures, without obligation, or a devastating compliment. Financial services sales-people give away a 'free financial overhaul' – isn't that kind of them? – before suggesting you may like to purchase a heavily commissioned pension or insurance policy in return.

These gifts are all the more potent when they are unexpected. Analysis of hypnotic techniques shows that it is much easier to encourage people to do things in a hypnotic state if they are surprised or shocked just beforehand. This is because when we are surprised or shocked we momentarily drop our defences. A lot of us operate under the maxim that

'You don't get owt for nowt in life', so when we're given something free and unexpected, and experience pleasure as a result, the odds are that we will feel strongly obligated to reciprocate. The free gift at the cosmetics counter is much more effective if it's unexpected, rather than something that customers come to expect as a right and a ritual. Hence companies using it as a ploy unpredictably and periodically.

The timing of the gift and the attached value placed on it are critical. Martin works for a private bank, where he developed a programme to coach bankers to sell their services to very wealthy clients:

> One of the things we noticed was how the handling of the brochures was often overlooked. We watched one female manager, who was excellent in all other aspects of her presentation. She came into the room where eight potential clients were sat round the table. Her greeting was friendly and professional, and then very quickly she flung copies of our very expensive brochure in front of them, with a 'Here's our little brochure for you to go away with'. Her whole handling and timing of the written material diminished its value. We now suggest these brochures are handed out at the end of the pitch, and handled almost with reverence to make them seem valuable. After all, they represent tangibly the value we feel we offer in our service.

A few years ago I worked for Levi-Strauss, who had a very charismatic Swedish marketing director.

During rehearsals for presentations of the new ranges, he would yell at the presenters, 'Make *l-o-o-v-v-e* to the jeans, make *l-o-o-v-v-e* to them.' You probably gather 'twas not his intention that the presenters should start embracing the garments. Instead he meant that they should be held and moved and folded as though they were very precious items. In relating to the garments this way, the presenters instructed their audience to attach great value to them. A powerful technique and the more so for being something that very few of the audience would consciously note.

Networking is all about the law of reciprocity. This is an idea that is often talked about rather mysteriously, and people write books and run courses on it, as though there is some great secret to it. What it's about – plain and simple – is trading: you scratch my back and I'll scratch yours. When it doesn't work it's usually because people don't understand this and are not upfront enough about the reciprocal nature of the activity.

Canny use, then, of this law means that you are aware when people give you something that you may be expected to reciprocate. And if you do not wish to reciprocate, you may need to make this clear, so that their unspoken expectation does not prevail. It also means that you can use the fact that others expect they should reciprocate to get what you are after.

Instantly irresistible

- Identify movers and shakers in the environment you want to excel in. Look for opportunities to do them favours and give them things. But maintain your self-respect.
- You're doing someone a favour, or giving them something, and you're not sure how tuned in they are to the idea that this is trade. When you do the giving, make a teasing comment along the lines of 'Now I wonder when you'll be able to scratch my back'.
- Never give people gifts with an apologetic 'It's just something very small'. It belittles you, the item and the person receiving the gift. Present it as though a lot of care and attention has gone into its procurement. Even if this isn't the case, the gift will gain attached value.
- Let the person on the receiving end really see your pleasure at what you're doing for, or giving, them. Hey, they could also feel like that soon on the return match!
- If someone owes you and they haven't been in touch for a long time, take the initiative yourself. Phone them for a chat. Remind them of their obligation to you by alluding to something that will make your favour or gift spring to mind. Give them a gentle reminder that you're 'owed one'.
- When you want somebody who's obligated to you to do something very specific, ask them. If they refuse, take them off your Christmas card list immediately. They're not playing the game.

- Under pressure from someone using this law? Either refuse their favour or gift: 'No thanks, Dirk from accounts, I couldn't possibly be interested in dining at Le Caprice with you . . .' Or accept it, but make it clear that you are unable to reciprocate in the anticipated manner: 'Thanks, I'd love to come but I have to be home early as I've an early appointment at the STD clinic the following morning.'

Negotiating with this law

Negotiating in all sorts of situations revolves around giving and taking concessions. Your partner plays football every Saturday and you spend as many Sundays as you can in the garden. Your fifteen-year-old son can stay out till midnight provided he cleans and tidies his room once a week. Your employer expects you to work very hard – but they give you a decent salary, private health insurance, a company BMW and a cheap mortgage.

We can use this idea of reciprocating concessions to get what we want. You go and ask your chief executive if you can be managing director of your division and she turns you down. You accept this refusal with good grace; you are philosophical and positive about it. You understand why she should refuse. What you're giving her now, of course, is a concession. You will not make her feel bad for what she's done. In the circumstances, you've done her a favour.

Two weeks later, when you come back to see her with a request to become marketing director of your division, she feels obligated to you for this favour. You get the gist.

> ### Instantly irresistible
>
> - If you're making a request to someone, and you suspect they may be resistant to it, then you could try deliberately asking for something more outrageous than you want initially. Respond to their horror at your request with good grace, and leave them feeling obligated to give you what you really are after.

2. The law of comparison

In the example I've just given you, someone making an extreme request and then making what seems like a much more reasonable one, another law is operating – the law of comparison. This says that to know what anything is we have to compare it with something else. So I'm wearing a navy blue jumper today, and not being colour-blind, I know it's navy blue because it's not black and it's not brown. But if I didn't have concepts of other colours, then I wouldn't be able to define the colour of my sweater.

We experience everything in its context, and that context will always involve ideas about how things are similar and how they are different. Our judgement of people, properties, the cost of things is relative to our previous experience and comparisons. Let's imagine you're recruiting a PA, and you see three candidates who you would judge with a C grade. Then along comes Ms Efficient who you would in isolation judge as a B+. Your judgement of lucky Ms Efficient is affected by your comparison of her with the three previous candidates. She seems even better than she is and you judge her to be an A.

Watch out for this technique if you are property hunting. Estate agents will often show you their poorer properties first, so that when you see a desirable and – funnily enough – much more expensive property, it seems all the more desirable. Some unscrupulous agents even have 'set-up' properties: not very desirable houses that they own. They'll show these to unsuspecting clients first, in order to bait them to buy the subsequent houses on offer.

If it's designer clothes you're after, the same law will apply. Skilled salespeople will always try to sell you the expensive suit or coat first, and then suggest you buy garments like shirts, sweaters and accessories. Why, that Gucci scarf for £500 seems a positive snip compared to the £2000 you've already decided to spend on the suit. But if you'd parted with £500 on the scarf first and then been shown the suit, it would have seemed like an awful lot more.

Being aware of the law of comparison can help make you much more irresistible. You're going to the wine bar with the aim of, um, meeting people, with friend A who dresses like a siren and friend B who is a sweater and sneakers sort of girl. Do I have to tell you which one you should sit by? (And yes, it isn't in the middle . . .)

Instantly irresistible

We can also use this law more tactically:

- When you're going for internal promotion, find out who else is going for interview. Chat to them about their interview time. Judging Zelda from sales and marketing to be a no-hope candidate, you'd be wise to schedule your interview to be immediately after hers. You will maximise your chance of dazzling.
- You want to be irresistible in a meeting and push something through. Either create a much more extreme proposal to be on the agenda prior to yours, or follow an extreme one that is already in the schedule. Your suggestion will seem much more reasonable by comparison.
- On the receiving end of manipulative 'compliance practitioners' using this law to influence you, stall your decision. Take the image of the house, or the time share or the garment home with you and visualise it in a different context, divorced from the comparison you saw it with. List objective plus and minus reasons for the choice, and make your decision on those.
- When you're choosing someone for a role or a job, and you are comparing several different applicants, create a scale of one to ten, with five being absolutely average, as a measure of what you are looking for. When you have a run of very good or very bad candidates, and then a contrast, use your central measure of average to assess them fairly.

3. The law of consistency

This law says that we like to keep our thoughts, our beliefs and actions consistent with what we have already done or decided. Consistency is viewed as a highly desirable attribute of an individual's self-image. It's often regarded as a cardinal sin to change one's mind and to appear inconsistent, even though we live in such a volatile world, where to do so might be the wisest course of action. When Neil Kinnock, for example, was leader of the British Labour Party, the press criticised him strongly for changing his mind. (My view – for what it's worth – is that we Celtic people do not share the need and concern for fixity that the rest of you do.)

But seriously, most of us like to feel that we have integrity, and part of this feeling comes from a sense that we are consistent and reliable. Businesses exploit this need for consistency by linking it to commitment. Sales training exploits this idea by training salespeople in a series of questions, which are all likely to be answered with a 'yes':

'It's a lovely day isn't it?' 'Yes.' 'Are you looking for a suit?' 'Yes.' 'This shade would really complement your lovely colouring. Does it appeal?' 'Yes.' 'Would you like to try it on?' 'Yes, please.'

And then they hope you will remain mindlessly consistent and when you come out of the fitting room and look in the mirror, they say:

'Oh, that looks fantastic! Are you going to take it?'

'You will, of course, answer:
'Yes.'
'*Yippee!*' thinks the salesperson, considering their commission.

We're subjecting ourselves to this law, as well as the law of reciprocity, when we take and use free samples from cosmetics companies. Having made a small commitment to using their moisturiser, the idea is that next time we want to buy a moisturiser we will seek to act consistently with this commitment and part with the necessary spondoolicks.

In his book, *Influence*, Robert Cialdini cites examples of toy manufacturers using this law. Before Christmas, toy manufacturers will advertise certain products extensively and usually plant some PR stories about it being impossible to buy a Teletubby, Furby or Buzz Lightyear. They will deliberately under-supply shops to create demand. Meanwhile, desperate parents, having promised little Sybil or Robert the offending toy, will be searching relentlessly to locate one. Many will be disappointed – the toy manufacturers will see to that.

Then, magically, after Christmas, these in-demand toys will reappear in the shops which are still doing roaring trade from Sybil and Robert's parents who are determined to keep their commitment to their offspring and to be consistent. When Mummy and Daddy are consistent, Sybil and Robert will learn to be so, too. They promised them the toy, so they will jolly well get it. Even though it's after Christmas and the playroom can't hold any more toys . . .

Unscrupulous car salespersons will use this law, too. A very low price will be offered on a vehicle and as soon as the unsuspecting customer shows some interest, they will be offered a test drive. This will engage their commitment. What usually happens then is that the low price that's been originally quoted turns out not to include air conditioning, heating, a radio, an aerial or perhaps even a steering wheel. And the hapless customer, having made some commitment to the vehicle and wanting to stay consistent, will end up forking out for all these 'extras'.

The law of consistency is used a lot as a prelude to selling. For instance, a financial salesperson will often conduct a thorough review of your finances. This will involve identifying financial goals you have and products you think you might need. There will be form-filling and signatures involved. Having made this agreement to let them advise you, you are far more likely to buy services from them – involving more form-filling and signing – than if you hadn't made the agreement.

In the same way, sales agreements for goods like televisions, video players and computers will ensure the minimum number of cancellations. Customers who get home and change their mind are far less likely to do something about it, when they've made that initial commitment.

Charities also use this law in telephone appeals.

When a fund-raiser calls you to ask you how you would respond to a request for a donation to that charity, and then calls you a few days later with the actual request, she maximises the chances that you will give. Having made that first commitment, you will wish to remain consistent.

And the law is used in election campaigns. Political parties spend a great deal of time and person power leading up to elections canvassing the general public as to how they will be voting. While this provides them with research, it also means that those who pledge their commitment verbally are more likely to get themselves down to the polling booths than those who had not verbalised their intentions.

We are most affected by commitments when we believe we take decisions with free will, without outside pressure. Highly sophisticated selling will offer the customer a range of options, about which they will believe themselves to be educated, but not pressurised. Although the options are likely to be positioned so that we find one more appealing than the others, we will be most committed to our decision when we believe that we've been left to our devices to make it.

Instantly irresistible

- If you want to change something about yourself or set yourself some goals, write them down. You are much more likely to achieve them when you've made this commitment.

- When you want somebody to demonstrate a certain quality towards you – generosity, understanding, punctuality, say – reminding them of how they've demonstrated it in the past may cause them to act in a consistent way. This is especially effective if the quality you remind them of is one that is very dear to them in terms of their self-image.

- This law suggests that the best people to ask for favours are the ones who've shown them to you previously. Having shown you a kindness once, they will be more likely to show you one again, in order to remain consistent. Don't push your luck with this one, though – repeatedly asking the same person for favours may bring an abrupt end to the friendship.

- Here's a job-finding technique that is hugely effective. Write a description of yourself on one sheet of paper. Show it to anyone who might be able to influence other people to give you a job. Ask them for their views of the description and anything they think you should change, add in or leave out. Thank them very much after they've done it. The odds are that having made this initial commitment to you in acting in your interests, they will act consistently and remember you when any opportunities are mentioned – either up front or in passing.

- Want to resist this law? Then practise saying 'no' or delay making any initial commitments. If you're not sure about the television or the computer the forceful salesperson is showing you, don't sign a sales agreement. When asked if you're looking for anything in particular, explain that you are 'just looking'.

- Under a great deal of pressure from this law, with someone reminding you of a previous course of action you took, with which you should be seen to be consistent? No way out of it, other than to argue that circumstances and the environment have changed, or to confess that you are a strangely mercurial, mysterious, unpredictable creature who makes decisions based on whimsy . . . and for whom consistency is not a priority. Shocking to others, but it works.

4. The law of social proof

This is the 'everybody's doing it' law. This explains rollerblading as a craze, the popularity of Delia Smith and why people pay inflated prices for designer clothes publicised by famous models and celebrities. It's all about endorsement. When a lot of people buy into something and endorse it, those of us who are keen on fitting in and being part of a big trend will go along with the trend. Others among us will be much more selective about their association – finding mass popularity a complete turn-off, but buying into trends that we believe just a select few are endorsing.

So demand for, say, Delia Smith's latest offering increases the more we read in the press that bookshops cannot meet all the requests for her books. Cosmetics PR in magazines constantly makes reference to filmstars or supermodels who use the latest product under promotion. New books have 'puffs' from well-known authors in the same field on their covers which always say how much they loved the book.

People like to back the horse that others are putting their money on, so at election time, for example, predicted outcomes in the press can be highly influential. In this context, this law explains the 'landslide victory', where polling for a particular party is considerably higher than the expected, because all the 'don't knows' at the last minute decide to back the winner. Some of the glory of victory then rubs off on them.

Innovative mail-order company director Johnny Boden understands the power of endorsement from people, and also the extent to which customers identify with endorsement. He uses real people in his brochures, with their Christian names and job descriptions. He sells his high-quality casual wear to customers who see it modelled by 'people like them', giving very strong social proof.

This law works in some quite serious contexts. There have been many instances of people being mugged or robbed or having accidents in cities, where passers-by do nothing for quite some time. This is explained by social proof, the thinking being: 'Nobody else around is doing anything so why should I?'

The 'Werther Effect' is named after a book by Goethe, where the hero commits suicide and lots of others copy him. It demonstrates that a highly publicised suicide is always followed by lots of copycat ones. Even scarier, there is persuasive data in the USA to show that after a highly publicised suicide, traffic and air fatalities show a consistent and significant rise. The spooky explanation for this is that some of these drivers and pilots were predisposed to be suicidal, and the reported event triggers off this urge. The persuasive nature of 'everyone's doing it' also explains how people behave in cults, and why horrible instances such as the mass suicide of hundreds of cult-leader Jim Jones' followers in Guyana occur.

But back to cheerier matters – you. Here's how to use this law to increase your irresistibility:

Instantly irresistible

- Do enough people know about your advanced diploma in topiary and your command of Balkan languages? Seriously, though, people are unduly impressed by formal qualifications, as those of us who've got a few of them quickly come to realise.
- Where have you been and who have you associated with that impresses people? A friend of mine

was fond of alluding frequently to 'When I was in Oxford . . .' What nobody knew, of course, was that he meant what used to be the polytechnic. He was not named Jeffrey Archer.

- But it's most important to be selectively impressive. If you try to impress too hard with lots of social proof, people will think you're desperate. Citing too many instances of social proof may create the impression that we are entirely dependent on external endorsement and have no self-belief. Much better to judge what your target values and then to drop in a chance comment that illustrates social proof they will be impressed by.
- When you're actively looking for a break or a job change, you might want to call in favours from all those influential people that you've been doing them for. Get them to write testimonials or make phone calls to act as referees on your behalf.
- To resist the law, just remember that because everyone's buying something or following a trend it doesn't mean it's a good thing. After all, in Britain the majority of voters repeatedly voted for a Conservative government throughout the 1980s.

5. The law of scarcity

This is the law of playing hard to get, which says that if we want something and we know its availability is limited, then we will want it even more. As G.K. Chesterton said: 'The way to love anything is to realise that it might be lost.' Fendi bags, Gucci loafers, Nicky Clarke haircuts all increase in value and desirability when we read – usually as a PR puff – that they are very hard to come by and involve three-month waiting lists.

Very often, sales are boosted by a combination of the laws of social proof and scarcity. We'll buy products because they combine endorsement from movers and shakers with being in short supply. The unscrupulous estate agent will use this one. She or he will indicate that a doctor who is moving into the area has seen the property and likes it a lot. This will alarm the prospective buyer into making an offer.

At the time of writing I am being offered a great opportunity to do field work on this subject as it coincides with my family selling one property and buying two others. We have just bought a house in Wales fairly hastily, because 'someone else from London has seen it and is making an offer'. I've no idea whether it was a scam or not. So reader, do as I say, rather than as I do.

When things are hard to get, they acquire greater value. It's quite understandable how members of certain professions with long apprenticeships – doctors, lawyers, psychoanalysts or London cab drivers – become enormously protective of their professional standing. The same goes for partners in accountancy and consultancy firms. Having worked so hard and for so long to achieve this status, it becomes extremely valuable to them when they eventually reach it.

Things become especially sought after when they've been in abundant supply, but have become much rarer. This has been the case with several friends of mine, who've decided to have a portfolio of part-time careers. They have been apprehensive about telling their customers and clients that they are limiting their availability, but they have been pleasantly surprised to find that their available time is more sought after than ever.

Salespeople often overlook the fact that when a customer's free choice is limited, they may well want to exert it more. You go into a shop looking for a particular item. The salesperson tells you they don't have it, they just have one alternative. You sensibly decide to go elsewhere. The clever salesperson will do whatever they can to help you get the original item, while also indicating to you what other alternatives are available. They will maximise your feeling that you are free to choose.

Instantly irresistible

- Read widely to spot trends. When new jobs emerge – fairly recent ones include nurse practitioner, web-site designer, personal trainer – they are usually in short supply. Set yourself up now to run a lifestyle-management company – organising out-of-work lives for busy people, or a home-shopping service that gets all the household's needs for them.

- Desperation is a massive turn-off. Sometimes, suggesting to your boss that you'd like to have a go at another job for six months, say – restricting your time and effort – may be a much more attractive prospect than prostrating yourself at his or her feet in order to get the role for life.
- Get unusual combinations of skills together – combinations that are very rare. A friend of mine is a Bulgarian-speaking economist, probably the only one in this country, and always in demand. I've been a voice teacher and a psychologist – and I know I've got jobs, sometimes, largely on the strength of this unusual combination. Some combinations just cry out to be tried: web-site designer and IT instructor (a dream for small businesses); nanny, housekeeper, bill payer, house and cat caretaker – a household manager, if you like – indispensable for the busy family.
- Resist this law by taking a break to rationalise. When you're in that car showroom and the salesperson says, 'It's the only model left and it'll be gone by this afternoon,' go outside, walk up and down, take a few slow breaths and remind yourself that there are seven other Saab dealers in the South of England.

6. The law of liking

This is a glaringly obvious law – we allow ourselves to be influenced by people we like and find attractive. So financial services advisors will be trained to approach all of their friends to start with. But let's be a little more explicit about what makes us like others:

We like people who are physically attractive. And there's a great deal we can all do to make ourselves physically attractive. Clichéd, I know, but if you feel good, you take care of yourself, eat well, and treat yourself physically and psychologically with respect, this will make you look good, too. Boost yourself with a good haircut and nice clothes. Plastic surgery aside, you may not be able to do much about your genetic inheritance, but you can draw attention to those good points and play down the bad. If you can't work out what these are, get some advice from a recommended image consultant.

It's worth it. All the research shows that attractive people earn more, get an easier time in court and get voted into office. So, when necessary, make sure you scrub up well.

We like people who are similar to us, who have things in common with us. And in order to convey that we are similar to others, we have to be able to make a quick assessment of them. This means doing very confident things like listening, and focussing all our attention on them. More of this in the next chapter.

We like people who remind us of ourselves because they endorse us, and bolster our self-images. This guideline is a good one to follow when making important decisions, such as what to wear for a first date or a job interview. Your prospective boss, or date, come to that, may be a 55-year-old, pin-striped-suit City hooray and you may be a fancy-free 25-year-old with a penchant for cropped tops and fatigues. If you want to emphasise things you have in common, it's best to dust down that dark tailored suit and put on those Bally pumps.

We like people who give us compliments. Even the toughest, most ruthless corporate warrior needs to be appreciated. In Britain, we are rather reticent about giving compliments – we don't like to be seen to be 'brown-nosing' or 'smarming'. But compliments are generous acts and, if genuinely meant, give people a great boost. They show others that you are able to focus your attention on them.

Always compliment others as specifically as possible. Rather than 'You look great', say 'That colour shirt really suits your eyes'. On the receiving end of compliments, some of us get embarrassed because we're not used to giving ourselves praise. So we rebut the compliment with a 'This old thing? I bought it secondhand.' The sub-text of this to the generous individual who has given you the compliment is 'I'm returning your kind act and diminishing it'. Much better to graciously accept the compliment. Who knows, you may open the floodgates for a whole lot more.

We like things and people that are familiar. So always take it as a compliment when someone tells you that you remind them of their mother or their ex-husband. Generally speaking, human beings find change unsettling, especially the older they get.

And while it takes them a while to adapt to new experiences and people, and their defences may be aroused, the familiar remains safe.

In some situations, this makes the case for a cosy, informal style of presenting yourself, where your main aim is to make other people feel comfortable with you. It's very useful, for example, if you're selling a service to others. Factor in here, though, that in some parts of working life, people are still very old-school-tie and formal. Like Lord King, who judged Richard Branson to be no threat at all because of his beard and sweaters.

In the past decade, businesses have latched on to the value of this guideline with customer service initiatives emphasising the value of long-term relationships and repeat business from satisfied customers familiar with the offerings.

We like people who co-operate with us. Obviously. Some individuals get very hung up on asserting their individuality over us, and to do this relentlessly disagree and challenge. It goes without saying that challenging and disagreeing can be very constructive at honing ideas and getting to the heart of issues, but the need I'm describing here is much more to do with the individual's ego.

Henry was a management consultant who was a newly appointed head of his division. He had a great deal of experience and success in selling roles. He was bullish and dynamic. He wanted his division to be massively successful.

Henry had asked for some coaching to build

more effective relationships with chief executives. When I went to see him, to talk about how we might approach this, I was amused to note that every utterance of mine was greeted with a judgement. Along the lines of 'a good idea'; 'Oh, I'm not sure about that' and 'I wouldn't agree with that'. After about ten minutes I asked Henry if this was how he would normally chat with chief executives. 'Yes, of course,' he replies. 'Is there anything wrong with it?' He had no idea that repeatedly passing judgement on his prospective client's expressions and ideas would be in any way detrimental to trust and relationship-building. He didn't realise that he would be better liked and provide a far better basis for a long-term relationship if he was much more co-operative. Henry had a lot of work to do . . .

We like people who are associated with the positive. Between the ages of about thirteen and twenty-five, I always wanted to be 'cool', and able to affect a sceptical disdain for most things. I'm naturally very enthusiastic so this stance was very difficult to achieve. Then, in my mid-twenties, I realised that being enthusiastic wasn't such a bad thing, and that other people seemed to quite like it. It's served me very well ever since.

People who have more of a positive attitude than a negative one are much easier to be with. Generally speaking, they live longer, too. We also like being associated with winners – with people who've done and achieved interesting things in life, sometimes against the odds. This means feeling comfortable letting people know about our past successes. We look at this in greater detail later.

If you've developed the habit of affecting a 'cool' stance a lot of the time, this may be detracting from your irresistibility. Get practising acting enthusiastic. Even if it's just about what's really hip.

Instantly irresistible

- So if someone who looks like George Clooney or Gwyneth Paltrow says they've got a great deal in common with you, and compliments you on your lovely eyes, and chats to you in a cosy familiar way, and is really helpful about any form-filling you have to do, and tremendously enthusiastic about life in general, then tries to sell you a pension – well, you can't say you weren't warned . . .

---

7. The law of authority

Many experiments in social psychology have demonstrated that we underestimate the extent to which we are influenced by authority. And that means authority conveyed both through behaviour, and how people present themselves and the words they use. Perhaps the most famous of these experiments was carried out by the researcher Stanley Milgram in the 1960s.

Authority figures, wearing white coats, issued directions to a group of subjects who were to act as torturers. The torturers believed they were administering the electric shocks as part of an experiment to study how punishment affects learning. No shock was actually administered but the torturers were assured that the shocks, although extremely painful, would cause no permanent damage.

The authority figures encouraged the torturers to keep administering the shocks even when they were flagging. While many of them became very stressed during the experiment, *all* of them raised the voltage to 300 volts, a level marked very strong. They heard at this point the simulated sounds of the victims pounding on the walls in pain. Even so, a further twenty-six out of the forty torturers, under instruction from the authority figures, took the voltage up another fifty percent again, to a horrendous 450 volts. The prediction by the researchers had been that only one in a thousand people would go this far. Interestingly, when the experiment was run using phone directions, rather than having the authority figures present, only nine out of the forty obeyed. So the experiment seemed to show that people are scarily responsive to authority figures – significantly so when they are physically present.

Bill Clinton understands the extent to which people are influenced by encountering authority figures in the flesh. During one of the many elections he has fought during his career, he was standing for governorship of Arkansas, where, a week before, all the indicators were that he would lose. This did not deter the comeback-kid. He got up every morning at 4.00 am and travelled around the state, meeting as many of the electorate as he possibly could, putting in a week's worth of punishing twenty-hour days. I bet you can guess what the result was. He won, of course.

But hey, I hear you think, how can this work for me? Well sorry, but to an extent I'm going to delay your gratification, because the subsequent chapter will be dealing with authoritative behaviour. But in the meantime here are some other ideas:

Instantly irresistible

- You will significantly increase your irresistibility in the marketplace if you are an authority on something people always need and want, or will have a greater need for in the future. So anyone who's an authority on sex, confidence, food, making money, good relationships, IT skills and has half-decent communication skills should be able to find a niche for themselves. (If you're thinking of becoming a television chef just remember that markets can get saturated.)

  Taking a gamble on future trends, you could start to become an authority on working effectively from home, being old but fit and happy, motivation based on quality-of-life priorities, quick and healthy organic eating, or looking smart but casual at work.

- While there are jobs, like television newsreading, which depend on authoritative behaviour alone, in most other contexts it's better to speak with genuine authority. You may be under the impression that to become an authority you need to reinvent yourself completely. This may not be necessary. What is it that you already know something about and how can you build on it? What you already know may not have been formally acquired. Interest and study in psychology turned out to be a good choice for me, because I built on what I'd learned from dysfunctional members of my family.

- The quiet confidence that comes from knowing you're an authority, rather than just acting like one, is really worth acquiring. Otherwise you'll always be worrying somewhere inside that you're going to be found out. Your options are always a lot wider when you can exercise real authority. Believe me.
- Just because that estate agent is dressed and behaving in the manner of the prime minister, remember it could all be costume and acting. You don't have to do what he says.

So that's it – seven powerful laws of irresistibility that can be used in all sorts of contexts. Experiment and have fun with them. Now on to the promised insights into irresistible behaviour.

4

Compelling Behaviour

I reckon Tony Blair's got charisma. Whatever else you may think he lacks – consistency or idealism possibly – his charisma is undeniable. Unlike his predecessor John Major, whose reputation suffered via the misdeeds of his fellow cabinet members, Tony always comes up smelling of roses – red ones, of course. There is something about him that people of all sorts – not just dyed-in-the-wool Labour voters – find completely irresistible. Much of this chapter will be about what that magical something is. We will by analysing behaviour that compels.

When we analyse behaviour signals, both our own and other people's, it can make us more versatile. We can identify our limiting patterns and change them. We can clarify what it is about other people's mannerisms that we like or find off-putting, and identify what character traits we associate with these mannerisms. When we understand how behaviour signals work, we can use them to influence how others think and feel – indeed, to make ourselves irresistible to them.

Social psychologists have carried out a lot of research into the impact we make on one another. As you're almost certainly aware, how we behave tends to have much more significance on other people than the words we use. This is especially true of a first encounter, where psychology professor Albert Mehrabian concluded that we judge one another 55 percent on what we see, 38 percent on what we hear, that is, the sound of a person's voice, and just 7 percent on the words they use. Do remember that this is a general statistic and may not apply to you as an individual. Perhaps you tune in far more to voice signals, or attach much significance to how a person uses words.

Now we might expect that when we get to know someone a bit better, they tend to pay more attention to our words. Not necessarily. Ray Birdswhistle, an American researcher, revealed that in conversation 65 percent of the meaning is gathered through visual signals – whether we know the other person well or not. But the amount of attention we pay to others' behaviour compared to what they're saying will be subject to all sorts of influences – our gender, for one.

Lots of social science studies have shown that women tend to pay more attention to behaviour signals than men. This explains what's often described as 'female intuition'. More women than men focus their attention on behaviour signals to interpret meaning. To male readers who are screaming 'not me' please remember this is a *general* finding – and lots of you, fortunately, will defy the norm.

Power play

A biological explanation for female sensitivity says that our brains are different from male brains. The two hemispheres of brain have different functions – one side handling emotions and sensitivity, the other concerned with analysis and language. In female brains the connections between these two hemispheres are larger, allowing for quicker transport from one side to the other.

In contrast, feminist sociology would say that it's all down to the history of power distribution. Just like the slave and master relationship, if men were powerful and dominated women, then women would need to pay more attention to male signals, as indicators of intention, than men would need to. After all, the male could determine a woman's fate. If he chose not to go out hunting, or got himself a new mistress to spend all his money on, then the dependent little woman would be in big trouble.

Presumably, if having less power means greater sensitivity, then other historically oppressed groups

– Jews, blacks and gays – would also experience it. But their reaction to what they observe may be different – they might go off and live separately, in ghettos, or develop their own strong and alternative cultures, or organise their own prosperous communities. Psychological research into minority groups and their reactions to behaviour seems consistent with the idea that it is just women who show this heightened sensitivity.

But back to what we're about here: individuals. When power is unequally distributed and abused – between the bullying boss and his PA, the oncology consultant and the cancerous patient, the dominating wife and the mousy husband – the weaker person will feel they need to be more sensitive to survive. Especially if the more powerful individual is volatile and prone to unpredictable moods.

In our family, my brother and I both tend to pay a great deal of attention to other people's signals. Our mother was plagued with something called a 'borderline personality disorder', which meant she suffered from unpredictable and dreadful moods. As children we would try to anticipate these storms by observing her behaviour. Maybe you have experience of a volatile personality where you've learned to do the same. Being rose-tinted spectacle wearers, my brother and I have decided that this increased sensitivity has served us well, in both our personal and professional lives.

Prejudiced first impressions

The trouble with making quick judgements based on first impressions is that while we human beings tend to regard ourselves as individuals, we very often quickly judge others in terms of groups to which they may belong. When we stereotype members of certain groups then we will judge with prejudice.

Let's say you've had a particularly bad experience with a 28-year-old, six-foot-two Glaswegian male with a sharp haircut and a smart suit. (Yes, I know, for some of us, this is the stuff dreams are made of). You meet Jack for the first time, who is a 29-year-old six-footer from Edinburgh, who works as a lawyer and dresses like one. Immediately, you think 'Ah, there's one of those', and your suspicions are raised. You generalise from past experience and judge Jack with prejudice. You can only prevent this happening when you've rationalised your past experience, and regard that individual as an isolated example.

In today's world, especially, we have to judge on first impressions. We have to quickly select features about a person on which to base our decisions. We will decide how to respond to a person through those features. If we didn't do this, we would need far too much time to research all the people with whom we have to deal.

But when we use race, colour, size, or physical attractiveness as these features, we choose aspects over which the individual concerned has very little control. And we are almost certainly generalising in our thinking: using ideas like 'all Welsh people are untrustworthy' or 'all short people are power crazy', based on our past experiences or irrational beliefs we've assimilated. This is sloppy, superficial judgement-making.

Much better in terms of making decisions about people, and responding intuitively, to base your decisions on features over which the individual concerned does have control. Base your judgement on decisions they will have consciously taken about themselves. Dodgy haircuts, humorous ties, unkempt beards, the wearing of bright pink or lime green all mean trouble in my book. And when I tell myself not to be so bigoted and to ignore these instincts – well, you've guessed it – I'm always wrong. As Oscar Wilde said: 'Only fools don't judge by appearances.'

But it won't just be appearance that you will use to judge others. Their behaviour will count for a great deal, too, and sometimes this can be confusing. When we are uncertain about a person's meaning, when their words and behaviour seem to contradict – like the person who agrees to go along with something verbally but makes this agreement through gritted teeth and with tense, twitchy limbs – behaviour is a more reliable guideline to real response. This is because we exert less conscious control over our body language and voice than we do over our words. And although some people have very readable faces, more of us are practised at controlling our facial response than we are our body language. So in certain situations, we may suffer from what's called non-verbal leakage – giving away our real feelings to others.

When you're judging others, then, pay close attention to their actions. And when you find yourself in a tricky or nerve-wracking situation, be aware of how your behaviour signals need to support your apparent intention.

In this section, I've talked about the connection between how we communicate and what we communicate, especially in connection with first meetings. But I think the guideline holds good, too, for later stages in a relationship. If you're confused about how someone should be judged when there is contradiction between what a person says and their actions, remember that it is their actions that will reveal their real intentions. Actions *do* speak louder than words.

You mean, I've got to learn to act?!

Before studying psychology, I studied drama and worked as an actress for a few years. About to enter my fifth production of *Under Milk Wood*, I decided there had to be more to life and ended my thespian phase. I've been struck, many times since then, by the connections between drama and psychology.

I'm often hired to help people 'act' better at work – whether they are presenting, interviewing, handling difficult customers and clients, running meetings, doing appraisals or pitching for business. And in life there are all sorts of contexts where we are called upon to act in order to achieve things. As parents, we may be seething inside, but have to conceal these feelings in order to discipline our children constructively. We may be trying to raise money for a good cause, and have to project enthusiasm and purpose while feeling exhausted and under the weather. We may have to inspire other people at work to follow courses of action of which we are not entirely supportive ourselves.

And these days, because of the growth of media coverage in every line of business and profession, the top people in almost any walk of life have one foot in showbusiness. Top lawyers, surgeons, teachers, scientists and accountants, even, will spend some of their time presenting at conferences, publishing articles, and doing press and PR profiles. So reader, whether you like it or not, if you want to really go for it in your career, or just become adaptable in your professional and personal life, yes, you have to learn to act. If you really want to get noticed, then public performance is a great way to do it.

Now I can understand reservations about this. Somehow, it all feels a bit disingenuous, consciously analysing behaviour signals, and extending or changing one's use of them. It's 'unnatural', people often say. And while certain aspects of human nature are common to all and, perhaps therefore, 'natural', how we use these aspects will be affected greatly by individual genes, habit and conditioning. Just consider the differences in expressivity of cultures who live around the Mediterranean, and those who live in the Far East.

If we stuck with being 'natural' we probably wouldn't learn to speak. When we are young, a certain amount of language ability is innate – we learn to speak through copying others. It's often amusing to note how children copy parents' body language. Watch a six-year-old boy and his dad strolling along the pavement with the same swaggering gait.

People learning to act may also feel that they are somehow 'tricking' others. But, of course, what you see is never what you get in human behaviour. My four-year-old can charm the pants off people with his behaviour, in order to satisfy his clearly focussed goal of increasing his Thomas the Tank Engine collection. Influencing and manipulating are words that are very close in meaning: whether we are doing one or the other will depend on the integrity of the goals we are striving to achieve. We influence people with integrity when we get them to do things that are good for themselves and others, like giving to charity, for instance. We manipulate people slyly when we get them to do things that are not ultimately good for them – like persuading them to buy pensions that result in unexpectedly low funds.

And whether we feel influenced or manipulated

by others will depend on the same criteria. If you voted for Labour in the last election and you now judge that they are making a bad job of government, then you will have been manipulated to vote for them. If you voted for them and you consider them to be doing a grand job, then you will have allowed yourself to be influenced by them.

Life at work would be easier for a lot of people if the necessity to act was acknowledged, and if more people were open about it. One theory suggests that stress may be caused by people consistently and regularly having to act differently from how they feel – you know, the 'have a nice day' routine. Where people feel exploited by an employer or believe that their goals are questionable, then this feeling of having to act will be especially difficult to handle.

It's my view that many organisations would improve relations with their employees if the demand to act was openly acknowledged. And organisations could allow for the fact that people need to have space to express the opposite of how they may be required to act. So every branch of McDonalds could have a 'nasty room', where staff went to exorcise their feelings by being horrid to a punchbag effigy of a customer at the end of a shift.

Learning to act can be immensely beneficial. We very often find that if we act as though we are confident, then other people respond to us as though we *are*, so we start to feel differently about ourselves.

The feedback we get from others makes us feel differently about ourselves. Here's Marion's experience:

> In my early thirties, I decided I wanted to change from financial management and go into selling. The cosmetics company I worked for were rather nervous about this – they thought I was shooting myself in the foot, as I was efficient in my existing role. But I really felt that I could be a great saleswoman. The sales director was infected by my enthusiasm and prepared to send me on a couple of courses. I observed her and her star performers in action handling our most important accounts. I decided that as soon as I got to meet our customers, I would act as though I was already a member of this team. Although I was very nervous when I first started, I found – amazingly – that people responded to me as though I really was an experienced saleswoman. My enjoyment and promotion since has been considerable.

Instantly irresistible

- Stuck in a rut with who you are? Join a drama group or evening classes in order to develop your acting skills, meet some new people and literally 'take you out of yourself'.
- A role model means just that. Find someone who is already realising some of your ambitions, observe what they do, and then *act* as though you are them. Analyse the range of behaviour they use, and identify from this range the type of behaviour that you would feel comfortable using.

Acting skills – the internals

There are basically two approaches to learning to act. There is the traditional British approach based on getting to grips with the externals – get the physical appearance and sound of the character right and everything else follows. So, an actor like Laurence Olivier would have used this approach, working on the physical attributes of the character first. The alternative approach puts the emphasis on getting the internal thinking right, and is known as 'The Method'. This approach investigates the character's motivation, asks what the intention is behind the words, and considers aspects from the actor's own psychology that they can bring to the character. It's the approach that's used by most film actors.

The ideas referred to at the end of Chapter Two, on how to handle feeling self-conscious through running an internal monologue about what you are doing in the here and now, owe their origins to the Method approach. When actors are rehearsing a script using this approach, they will often go through the entire play deciding the intention, or the *subtext*, behind each line. 'Subtext' simply means the intention behind the line, and may be at odds with the words. Like a 'How are you?' delivered with the intention of dismissing the character on the receiving end.

Using this approach, actors consciously control

the way they think, in order to think *like the character*. We can use this idea to combat shyness and self-consciousness and to help ourselves behave in a way that others find compelling.

Clear internally, compelling externally

In Chapter Two, I talked a lot about how it is helpful to be conscious about what you are *doing* in situations where you might feel shy and self-conscious, rather than being preoccupied with what is being done to you – that is, whether people are judging you or rejecting you.

The most compelling type of behaviour that we can show other people is interest. In terms of intention, this means to involve, engage, consider and charm others. A friend, Sally, told me this story:

> When I was at university, there was a girl in my year that men seemed to swoon over. Yet she was not obviously attractive – dumpy, bespectacled and she dressed rather like a bluestocking, with a slightly nutty professor air about her. In passing I mentioned to my boyfriend that her charms were somewhat mysterious. 'Rubbish,' he replied, 'when you talk to her, she makes you feel like you are the only person in the world at that time, and that she finds you completely fascinating.'

And when we are interested in others, and become *other* focussed, it minimises the amount of attention we have available to be self-conscious and shy. We forget about ourselves, and give attention to others in a way that encourages the very best direct communication between human beings.

A seasoned campaigner like Bill Clinton understands compelling behaviour. He understands the power of other-focused behaviour. That's why he has spent huge amounts of time pressing flesh on the campaign trail. He meets so many people, it gets him elected.

Because I've been doing what I do for quite a while it means that I've been lucky enough – or unlucky enough, depending on your viewpoint – to observe three British prime ministers at fairly close quarters. Several years ago, I clocked Margaret Thatcher arriving at a hotel to launch her book, *The Downing Street Years*. She looked like she'd just come out of hair and make-up, and walked with a great sense of purpose. But *en route* she stopped continually to greet onlookers. Radiating charm, she'd enquire, 'How are you?' and make comments like, 'So good to see you.' She sent signals of being a woman with a mission, and someone who was very keen to endorse her relationship with the onlookers. It was an expert demonstration of other-focused behaviour.

Your role as researcher

One way to focus more attention on others, and to be less self-preoccupied, is to hold an idea of yourself as a researcher. What researchers do is to ask questions, so they focus on others and the environment with interest and enquiry. This idea of acting as a researcher is a useful one in all sorts of testing situations. Especially when we experience dread about a situation and, beforehand, start to create a self-fulfilling prophecy about it all going horribly wrong. If we view ourselves instead as a researcher, keeping an open, enquiring mind, we are less likely to guarantee a disastrous outcome.

Instantly irresistible

- Shy and self-conscious? When you next go to a social situation where there are lots of new people, view yourself as a researcher. Give yourself three research questions to which you want an answer: What's the average age of people here? How many are blond? Are many of them wearing spectacles? Now you may only manage to find answers to one or two of these to begin with, but over a period of time give yourself the project of getting answers to all three questions. Then set more probing questions that need to be answered, like 'What's the mood here, generally?' The effect of setting out to answer these questions should minimise the amount of attention you have available to worry about how you are being judged.
- When you are talking one-to-one, or one-to-two, with people, you can maintain an interest in others by thinking about questions like 'What interests this person?' 'What are they motivated by?' and

'What do they really care about?' This will help you to focus and direct the right kinds of questions and responses while you're talking.

Acting skills – the externals

This involves becoming conscious of, and changing, your external behaviour. We're talking here about the visuals – eye contact, facial expression, body language; and the auditory, which means controlling your voice, using pace, pitch and projection effectively, and keeping listeners enthralled.

We are often not aware of the extent to which we can change these signals: we don't know what our particular use of them conveys, and we allow them to become subject to mindless habit. We feel self-conscious making changes. Well, to change our external behaviour we have to become self-conscious in the very best sense of the word. Indeed there is an oft-quoted sequence about behaviour change involving a clever play on words:

- Before we decide to change something we are often unconsciously incompetent.
- When we decide to change something we become consciously incompetent.

- When we learn to do something new we become consciously competent.
- When we have really assimilated the new behaviour we become unconsciously competent.

While we change our behaviour, then, we may become very self-conscious about it. But fear not because, in my experience, people have to do very dramatic things to their behaviour, like changing accent dramatically, for others to notice. For the truth, dear reader, is that most of the time we are preoccupied with our own agendas. Only those of us who get paid for it tend to pay a great deal of attention to the detail and nuances of the behaviour of others.

Irresistible visuals

What we want to aim for here is a sense of 'I am quite comfortable with myself, and with other people looking at me'.

Eye to eye

We project confidence to others and increase our allure when we look at them. Pupils dilate when we see someone attractive. In days gone by, women used to put the herb belladonna in their eyes in order to make their pupils dilate, thereby making themselves more attractive to others. When we look at others when they're talking, we use that most irresistible of qualities – attentiveness. So do it lots, and accompany those attentive eyes with nods of the head, and encouraging *Mmns* and *yes, I sees*.

When you look at someone and are paying them lots of attention, you don't want to make your stare relentless. This will make you look as though you want to intimidate or dominate them – or as though you've imbibed some unusual chemical substance. Our eyes naturally and frequently move away from people's faces as we speak, which mirrors our brain activity. And it's not a bad thing to show evidence of brain activity.

People often ask me how long they should look at someone's face before moving their eyes elsewhere. It's impossible to prescribe a time period, such as three or four seconds. Your gaze needs to be long enough to register their facial expression and to show them that you are considering their reactions.

We avoid making eye contact with others when we are hyper-sensitive to their responses, feeling that they may be judging or rejecting us. So avoiding eye contact with others is often seen as an indicator of being self-effacing and lacking in confidence. When eye contact is very quick and darting, a person may be regarded as 'shifty'.

And sometimes, of course, a lack of eye contact goes with arrogance, in that the person has so little regard for the reception of others to what she says or does, that she doesn't need to clock it.

Shy people sometimes make the mistake of thinking that if they focus on something close to the other person's eyes, like their forehead, then they can cheat eye contact. Not so, I'm afraid. The resulting effect is likely to make the other person feel strangely disquieted by the idea that a piece of fluff or ink mark is lurking between their eyebrows.

Confident eye contact

To convey that most irresistible of qualities – confidence – through eye contact, it's helpful to become comfortable making lots of it, wherever you go. Get to meetings and parties early if you can, so that you can greet people individually as they arrive, almost in the role of hostess or host. On the divide-and-rule principle, it's always easier than addressing the whole group. You'll later find you are more comfortable mingling – after all, you've already created some rapport with individuals.

Be aware of making as much eye contact when you are speaking as you do when you are listening. The shy and self-effacing among us are often very generous in their eye contact when listening, but less generous when holding forth and being the centre of attention.

Sexy eye contact

A few years ago, I was asked to coach a world-famous, sex-symbol sportsman, who wanted to become a television presenter. A queue of my girl-friends formed offering their services as my assistant. And no, I'm not going to tell you who it was, because it's more than my reputation's worth.

I had never found this individual particularly attractive; I like my chaps a little more, *um*, craggy, but I was very interested to meet this sex god and observe him at close quarters. It was fascinating to notice that when he spoke to me and listened his eyes roved over my face and rested on my mouth. While I found this rather unnerving – did I need urgent orthodontics? I wondered – I realised that it was highly seductive behaviour. You might want to try this, but results are not guaranteed.

Instantly irresistible

- John Kennedy and Bill Clinton have more than just presidential and legendary seducer status in common. They both mastered a particular eye-contact technique. It involves looking at another individual, and moving your eyes from one eye to his or her other eye. This creates the impression that you really care about what makes them tick, and that you really want to see into their psyche.

Now how do I know this? Have I been lucky enough to be on the receiving end of this presidentially penetrating probe? No, 'fraid not. But both presidents perfected this technique in television broadcasts, gently moving their eyes from side to side as they looked at viewers. So millions of Americans would be left with the impression that their president really cared about them.

Best to be relatively sober when you try this one on someone you want to impress or seduce!

- Do bear in mind that when someone finds you irresistible they may avoid making eye contact with you, in case you spot those dilating pupils. So when you're in a meeting and Hubert from Operations is failing to make any eye contact with you at all, it's probably because he already finds you utterly *irresistible*.

An irresistible expression

There's just no chance of becoming irresistible if your face reads as though you are about to have your wisdom teeth pulled out without an anaesthetic. Generally speaking, facial expression doesn't get much attention in communication skills literature. This is a shame, because it's very important.

To look irresistible, we need to look relaxed – at ease and comfortable with ourselves. Other people will then be more inclined to feel at ease with us. You'll have noticed, I'm sure, that the face is a very common site of tension in humans. Just travel on a tube train during the rush hour when the carriage is very crowded, to see what I mean. You'll observe muscles in the sides of people's faces bunching up – their jaws tightly clenched – caused by the stress of being in such close proximity to others.

To an extent, all of our faces are masks behind which we conceal what we are thinking or feeling. Some of us mask a great deal, especially those of us who negotiate a fair bit, when inscrutability can be a very helpful behaviour. Or, as part of our jobs we might have to control demanding emotions. In my work, I often notice a marked degree of inscrutability among litigating solicitors, police officers and surgeons, for example.

For some of us, masking becomes so habitual that it can be very difficult to be expressive when we need to be. This limitation will not boost our irresistibility quotient. When we want to make ourselves or our cause influence others, we have to be able to project facially the appropriate expressions. Enthusiasm, passion and commitment are all highly intoxicating qualities with which to influence others. If you're talking these qualities, while your face is looking as though you're sucking a lemon, then you won't succeed. We trust people more when their facial expression seems to match their thoughts.

An enthusiastic expression is a great communication skill. Human beings are always inspired by ideas about *what could be*. That's why several million people in this country twice weekly commit the utterly irrational act of playing the lottery. It's not for the money – which by itself is a neutral commodity – it's for *what could be* with the money. So when you readily and warmly convey enthusiasm you appeal to *what could be*.

You can spot different levels of expressiveness working for and against candidates in election campaigns. Contrast say the style of ex-prime minister John Major and Tony Blair. John Major has a high degree of facial inscrutability. He had two expressions – a bland one and a smile. In comparison, Tony Blair shows quite a wide range of different facial expressions. The electorate perceives him to have greater vision and commitment as a result. Whether he's acting or genuinely feeling what he conveys, as long as his behaviour signals appear appropriate to the situation and genuinely felt, they will stand him in good stead.

Cultural and gender expectations will also affect how we use facial expressions. In the Far East, for instance, people tend to be far less expressive than we are in the West. Americans have a very smiley 'Have a nice day' culture. In Britain we do not have this to the same degree – yet.

There are many different expectations about facial expression, largely based on stereotyping. A study in America showed that when two groups of people, one male and one female, were observed, different judgements were passed. The men and women surveyed both smiled to the same degree. The group of people who were asked for their responses to these smiling individuals described the men as warm, intelligent, friendly and looking for fun. They described the women as warm, intelligent, friendly, looking for fun – and desperate to please. So the women who smiled a lot tended to be regarded as more eager to please and therefore less assertive than the men who smiled a similar amount.

What does this mean for you? Well, if you don't smile a great deal normally then grinning manically at all and sundry in order to increase your irresistibility is probably not wise. But there is a very noticeable difference between a tense expression and a relaxed one. Especially a relaxed face that reads 'I'm approachable'. If you want to perfect a dazzling, irresistible smile, bear in mind that this expression is as much about what happens around the eyes as the mouth. Thinking *I'm really pleased to see you* and looking in the mirror may be good practice for turning on one of these dazzlers at will.

Instantly irresistible

- Television newsreaders perform facial isometrics before they go on air. You can do the same if you want to relax your facial muscles. Stretch your face forward and backward, drop your jaw down. Have a good yawn, and blow out through the lips,

Dobbin-style. Chew around a bit with the lips. Remember, though, if you perform these activities on public transport, members of the constabulary may find you irresistible.

- Rather more mindfully, warm up your face before you go to the party, interview, meeting or presentation by running over the gist of what you're likely to be talking about, and over-enunciating. The cat can make a good rehearsal audience. When you do this, your muscles will be much more responsive to messages from your brain that say things like, *relax*, *smile* and *look pleased to be here.*

- An open, friendly expression will arise from an appropriate mental intention. So, in situations where you want to look pleasant, remind yourself that you are involving people, considering their reactions, and welcoming them. These are clear intentions you demonstrate through your behaviour towards others.

- Sometimes people are self-conscious about smiling because they've got bad teeth. Get them fixed! Uneven, grimy pegs ain't irresistible.

- Models and actresses get their lips looking irresistibly sexy in photographs by moistening them with saliva so they gleam, and by keeping their lips slightly open, suggesting kissability. Be warned – I've tried this a couple of times in snaps, and have ended up looking notably gormless. It's a technique that needs practice.

- When you want to present your best side to a camera, it's usually the side that corresponds with your dominant hand. You'll notice that the features on your dominant side are usually sharper and smaller. So, putting those to the forefront, closer to the lens, with the larger, softer features in the background, others will see a happy balance. Tempting though it may be, I wouldn't try this live, with people. They might think you're a little strange.

So that's how to get those features irresistible. Now let's look at how we get the body language to match.

Body language

Where irresistible means sexy, body language has to feature. Among people who run training courses, there's a guideline claiming that one way of keeping people interested in the programme is to mention sex every twenty minutes. I notice that when participants on my courses are looking somewhat jaded at my wittering on about the psychology of communication, they spring into life when I bring up the subject of body language. I'm sure this is because they know that when we find others attractive, it is our body language that is often the giveaway.

Revealing touches

We often give away that we may find somebody attractive through preening gestures: touches to the hair, strokes to the leg, that suggest we are checking our attractiveness or applying sensuality to ourselves, which we would like to share with others.

Some people use very blatant body language. Take the chap standing at a bar, chest puffed up, each thumb looped through a trouser waist loop, with his hands spread across his hips in a v-shape, fingers pointing in a downwards direction. Yes, you get the picture – he's indicating that you should pay attention to his willie or, as the experts would call it, using 'primate crotch display'.

But it's our eyes that really give us away when we find others attractive. Studied indifference will be interspersed with darting glances to check how the other person's reacting. These darting glances may be directed at the bits of the other person's anatomy we are most interested in. When we've captured their attention and started to talk with them, we are likely to gaze into their eyes for longer than usual, with the aforementioned pupils dilating frantically.

As a general guideline, our behaviour becomes more heightened when we fancy someone. We are likely to display our bodies more and to become more animated. Our head and hand gestures will become more expansive and energetic, we will laugh and smile more and – surprise, surprise – indulge in more 'tongue-play', moistening the lips more frequently and opening the mouth a bit more. All, I suppose, as the hors d'oeuvre to what we hope will be a memorable main course.

Language of confidence

Body language experts like to identify bits of body language – such as folded arms – and give these gestures universal meaning. The meaning that's most often ascribed to this gesture is that it is defensive and apologetic. But, in different contexts, folded arms may mean that the person is snuggling into a cosy conversation over the garden wall or giving themselves a reassuring cuddle. In any analysis of body language, the most we can hope to describe with any predictability is general guidelines. So, in this section I thought I'd describe guidelines for using body language that conveys those most irresistible of qualities – confidence and composure.

The first guideline is that some of us habitually use body language that encourages others to view us as significant beings. We will convey the impression that we are powerful, and comfortable with our authority. A lot of this will be about how we occupy space. Sitting back comfortably in a chair, your shoulders well back, your arms resting in your lap, your posture fairly expansive, taking up plenty of room, you will look a lot more powerful than if you round your shoulders, drop the top half of your body, making yourself look rather small and insignificant.

So, if you are seen to be comfortable taking up plenty of space, people will regard you as being confident. You'll notice the significance of the use of space in television interviews. Some interviewees will sit well back with their arms spread expansively on the chair arms. Others will lean forward, round their shoulders and drop their chins, in an apologetic style.

Another indicator others may read from our body language is about how open and accessible we appear, or in contrast, how closed and defensive. So, for instance, if you're walking round with your arms behind your back, and your head raised, while you may look rather military you will also look very confident. If you fold your arms very tightly around your body so that your hands are almost round your back, you will send out signals that almost say, 'As nobody else is giving me a cuddle, I'd better give myself one.' You may indicate to others that you are badly in need of reassurance.

Nervous fidgeting, too, with your cutlery over dinner, perhaps, or obvious nervous mannerisms like hair twiddling, detract from a confident and irresistible appearance. If you don't seem at ease with yourself, you won't be likely to make others feel that way.

The next guideline is perhaps slightly less obvious, but very interesting, in terms of influencing other people. And it's about demonstrating degrees of involvement or detachment through our body language. Consider an arrogant boss – we might see him spreadeagled backwards in his chair, arms raised with hands supporting his head which tilts backwards and his legs spread out wide apart in front of him. The expression on his face will be reading 'What have you got on offer? What can you do to entertain me?' His body language will be characterised by a detachment, disengagement and distance. People often adopt this pose because they are rewarded by seeing others feel slightly intimidated by it.

Some of us will spend a lot of time during our working day in detached, objective analysis. We may find that appearing detached often helps us achieve our goals in certain situations. The trouble is that we can forget that influencing others to find us irresistible is about engaging their hearts and imaginations, as well as their reasoning. We may rely on appearing coolly detached, just because it's worked well for us in the past when it's the wrong tactic.

On television, again, you see these differences in style. It's the difference between the television presenter who sits far back in their chair, is quite inscrutable and doesn't seem warm or involved with the viewers, and the presenter who leans forward, who is quite facially expressive, who uses their hands in an expressive way and seems to be chatting to the viewer in a very conversational style. Several years ago, I worked on the launch of a morning television station in this country, where, to much hype, a newsreader who was reading the ten o'clock evening news moved to present a new morning chat show. Clad in a pink suit, on a pink sofa, she just couldn't adapt her coolly objective 'news at ten' style to a more folksy, involved one. She was quickly replaced by a very expressive, involving presenter, Lorraine Kelly, who now has her own show.

To be able to convey at will that you're involved or detached in a situation is a great skill. Projecting enthusiasm and involvement will attract others to you and your cause. When you can calmly disengage from a situation, like a tough negotiation, at will, that can also be to your advantage. Coolness and detachment certainly have their place – especially when you want something that someone else is selling.

My family likes visiting antique fairs and a few months ago we went to a large one, where there were lots of good buys. Now it's not exactly relaxing taking two under-five boys into such an environment, but fortunately there was a café, where I spent much of our visit entertaining them. My partner took me over to a stall to look at a chest, by which time I was thoroughly fed up with the event and couldn't care less whether we bought anything or not. Rather out of character, I looked at the chest impassively and said, 'Yes, it's all right.' Clocking my reaction, the stallholder offered us a 25 percent discount. Try as I might, I probably won't be able to replicate that degree of disinterest in the future.

Informally appealing

Like anything else, there are trends in how we communicate, and we're in the age of 'Call me Tony', as the British prime minister announced at his first cabinet meeting. Informality and involvement prevail.

In testing situations, we may try as individuals to present a thoroughly too-good-to-be-true version of ourselves. We may become more formal, using our poshest accent and inhibited behaviour. Through the use of body language, symmetry equals formality. So if you sit in a meeting with your feet both flat on the floor, your hands folded neatly in your lap and your chin tilting demurely downwards, you will look much more formal than if you cross one leg over the other and lean on one arm of the chair, with your other hand resting in your lap, and with your head slightly tilted. Asymetry reads informal, relaxed and accessible. Standing, just putting slightly more weight on one foot than the other, can make a person seem much more relaxed.

Irresistible matching

Therapists and counsellors learn to match their clients' body language to facilitate rapport. Perhaps this is why so many women fall in love with their male therapists – that, and the fact that this may be the first time in their lives they've encountered a male who listens.

When we make ourselves behave in a way that is very similar to another person's, we flatter that person through endorsing their self-image. This explains why you often find partners who seem to look remarkably like one another – or dog owners who've chosen pets who look just like them.

You've got to be fairly subtle about this, though. I bet some of you have been on the receiving end of some poor sales training, in the way that I have, where an inept sales person clumsily mirrors your positioning and gestures. Rather than going for a direct imitation, it's subtler and more effective to *suggest* similarity. When they slump back, you might lean back; when they fold their arms, you might fold your hands in your lap, and when they cross their legs in your direction you might just move your feet on the floor towards them. Remember: sensitivity is the key here.

Instantly irresistible

- Sitting in front of a mirror, see how you look sitting well back in your chair, perhaps with one leg crossed over the other, your arms folded in your lap, your shoulders back, your head raised and a sense that you are taking up plenty of space. Now try a very different position with your arms folded tightly across the front of your body, your body tilting forward, and your head dropped. You'll notice a big difference in how you appear to others.

- If you find it quite difficult to remain engaged with others and to be expressive, then warm up physically beforehand. Shake out your arms and legs, get them moving, relax your shoulders by rolling them backwards a few times. Just get your body feeling looser so that when you go into a situation where you want it to express certain emotions, such as involvement, it's ready to respond.
- Practise beforehand the body language you will use in important situations. Video yourself if it helps. While you may feel very self-conscious, it will make you become helpfully self-aware. And, *in situ*, it will be one less thing to worry about – you'll know that you'll be sitting or standing in a way that conveys good signals.

Moody movement

The way we move can send out lots of signals about our confidence and composure. Under stress, human beings are said to experience a fight, flight or freeze response. The flight response is perhaps the one we see most often, where a person under pressure will rush around frantically in a quick, jerky manner. Their rushing will make them appear as if time is completely out of their control. If you have a tendency to do this, then the message is: slow down. When you look like you are trying too hard, people won't find you irresistible.

When we are under pressure, some of us become rather aggressive. We act on the fight response, thinking we'll stage a pre-emptive strike before anybody gets us. So we may find ourselves being quite aggressive in the use of our body language: wagging finger, thumping fist, thrusting chin . . . rather heavy deliberate movements. Again, if you demonstrate too much fight response, you might tempt other people to fight back, or indeed suggest to them that they should start behaving like naughty children because your behaviour is being inappropriately authoritarian. Alternatively, they can raise their hackles and become defensive.

And the freeze response usually occurs when somebody is very nervous in a situation and hasn't got his or her mind in gear beforehand. So, a couple of minutes into the interaction, they will suddenly startle like a rabbit caught in the headlights. If this is happening to you a lot, you need to do something about your time management and take time out beforehand to think things through in quiet.

Instantly irresistible

- Compelling behaviour involves the ability to convey at will relaxed stillness. If you find this difficult, yoga, relaxation exercises that involve squeezing and releasing different parts of the body, and even controlling your caffeine intake may help.

And now on to how to create irresistible sound.

Sounding irresistible

These days, a great deal of initial contact between people is made over the phone. And, yes, it is disappointing when that chocolate-brown velvety voice manifests itself in its physical entirety – and you discover that he's squat and bearded, with spots, halitosis and a zeal for computer games. But someone will love him – even if it's just for those dulcet tones.

Let's face it, if someone's thinking of spending a lifetime with you, or intending to employ you for several years, or intending to spend a lot of time with you discussing business, then a pleasant-sounding voice will be a great asset. But people become confused about their voices, regarding them to be something they're stuck with and can't do much about. This is probably because we can't see our voices in action.

People are also confused about the differences between voice, speech and accent. And in this country, where there's still a lot of snobbery, and inverted snobbery, about accent, how people sound tends to be a very sensitive subject. At the time of writing, there's been a recent and widespread outcry because the novelist Beryl Bainbridge, under the influence of a couple of sherbets, suggested that people from her native town, Liverpool, should do something to improve their accents.

Before becoming a psychologist, I was a voice teacher and, like many other voice teachers, my view is that whatever your accent, it's possible to have a well-produced speaking voice. Having said that, there's no use pretending that people are not prejudiced towards accent. John Honey's book, *Does Accent Matter?*, proved that it did – and that if you spoke with an uneducated Midlands accent you had the most unpopular British accent of all.

The ability to change accent depends on confidence, a good ear, and being able to identify and isolate different speech sounds. I've come across people who've changed accent almost completely (pitch patterns tend to remain) by immersing themselves in Radio 4, listening to it constantly and imitating the presenter's accents. Other people will have changed accent through a much more technical process of going to a voice teacher and having phonetic analysis done to identify which of the sounds they make are furthest removed from standard English. They'll have practised endless exercises which help them shift these sounds closer to standard English. But most people will not want to take their voice training quite so far.

Sounding in control

Voice is produced by breath striking the vocal cords, and the quality of our breathing determines how controlled and confident we sound. When we get stressed or very enthusiastic we often find that we breathe more quickly. Our breathing pattern shifts into the upper part of our chest and is characterised by audible gasps for breath and sometimes visible movement in the chest and shoulders.

To sound confident and relaxed, and to feel that we can project our voices when we want to, we have to know how to control our breathing. Breath is the fundamental power source of our voices. When we're in control of our breathing and getting maximum power for minimum effort, we let the breath drop low into the bottom of the lungs. There is about eight times as much capacity for oxygen in the lower part of the lungs as there is at the top. We sometimes snatch in breath quickly and un-helpfully because our conditioning tells us that we should take a deep breath in if we get into a diffi-cult situation. We often interpret this to mean a big breath that we suck in quickly with a lot of effort – and this becomes trapped in the top part of our lungs. We keep topping up our oxygen supplies this way, so that hits of oxygen get sent via the bloodstream to the brain. We get the 'mouth engaged but not connecting to mind sensation', which indicates we're putting ourselves on the path to hyperventilation. Very disquieting – and not at all irresistible.

Our delivery will sound strained, rushed and panicky as a result.

Instantly irresistible

- If you find yourself breathing rapidly through nerves of excitement and you'd prefer to keep cool, calm and in control, slow down your breathing rate by concentrating on breathing out slowly. But please continue to breathe in because no calming technique is worth dying for. Your body slows down your breathing automatically, of course, when you sigh. Slowing down your breathing rate will bring down your heart rate too. It should get rid of any nervous wobble in your voice.

Pacing it

The pace at which we speak has two aspects: the rate of delivery, how many words per minute we speak, and our use of pause. To keep people listening, and to sound enthusiastic, it's a good idea to speak fairly quickly. On average people speak at about 150 words per minute. When listening, our brains can process an incredible 450 words per minute. So unless you want to sound patronising and lose people's attention, it's a good idea to keep up the rate of delivery.

This doesn't mean, of course, that you need to sacrifice the pauses. By far and away the most useful voice technique is a comfortable use of pauses. When we pause effectively we create the impression that our brain is engaging before we speak. We create the impression that we're considering our listeners' need to assimilate what we're saying. And, if we pause when we're asked a question, we create the impression that the question was valuable and we need to think for a moment before we answer it. *Ums* and *ers* are often fillers for speakers who don't feel comfortable pausing. So stick a big PAUSE sign on your phone, if you need to do more of it and master this most useful of techniques.

I meet many people in my work who say they need to slow down when they get nervous. Almost all of them need to do this by becoming more comfortable using pauses.

The auditory cuddle

The best way to keep people listening is by varying your projection. If you listen to good newsreaders you'll notice that through an entire news bulletin they vary their projection quite a lot. This makes what we're hearing sound interesting and keeps us listening.

How does voice projection work? Well, the first thing you need to master is the breath control, which we've already talked about. The next thing you need to check is that you're not tensing in your throat, producing a strident tone. If your throat feels as though it's tightening, you can relax it by yawning, or sighing out on '*hoe*' '*haw*' or '*hee*'. Probably best to do this one alone.

Good voice projection works by moving the tongue, teeth and lips crisply and quickly. The very best way of developing a compelling sound is to think about confiding as you speak. Technically, this encourages us to relax in the throat but to be more energetic and precise in how we work our muscles as we articulate. This 'confiding' technique gives a voice an inviting and intimate quality which is quite irresistible. It's extremely flattering to our listeners because it creates the impression that whatever we are saying is just for them, personally. It's a mode of delivery that is the equivalent of an auditory cuddle.

I have no hesitation in recommending this as one of the most effective techniques in the book. If you're getting het up and you don't want to appear so, or you really want someone to retain what you're saying, then I recommend you use it. You can't use it all the time – or people will start to find listening to you hard work – so those cuddles have to be rationed.

Do listen to prime ministers, presidents and television newsreaders making use of this technique. Charismatic salespeople use it, too. Occasionally, people have said to me that it reminds them of Margaret Thatcher and they worry that they'll end up sounding patronising – it was Margaret Hilda's grandiloquent slowed-down delivery that created a patronising effect. You can auditorily cuddle your audience while keeping up the momentum and enthusiasm.

As I must do . . . so on to the next chapter.

5

The Case for You

As someone brought up in this country, odds are you'll feel uncomfortable talking about yourself. We British prize self-effacement and modesty. This partly explains how someone like the very self-effacing John Major can become prime minister. It is inconceivable that someone like him could become president of the USA. But then they have their own problems to do with that role, relating to dignity and appropriate behaviour.

Our cultural values reach us to varying degrees via our families. You, for example, may have been brought up in a family where you weren't encouraged to draw attention to yourself, or to crow on about your skills and achievements. When you did get exuberant about yourself, perhaps you were reprimanded severely for 'showing off'. This may make it extra-tough for you when you meet new people, when you have to go to job interviews, or when you're selling yourself or your services. To make ourselves irresistible to others in any of these contexts we have to become comfortable and confident talking about ourselves. In this chapter, I'll show you how.

Increasingly in the modern world, it's important to be able to converse with ease. A study of highly successful managers found that by far the greatest percentage of their time was spent in what they described as networking activities, by which they meant exchanging information and experiences with others both inside and outside their firms. With business becoming faster and faster, we often have a very short time to demonstrate to employers, clients and customers that what we've got on offer could be irresistible to them. These circumstances favour people who are open and uninhibited in talking about themselves. So the first section of this chapter is about making great conversation.

Of all the skills described in this book, the art of conversation is the most important to practise on a day-to-day basis. If we don't practise this skill regularly, we usually find ourselves being called upon to use it under pressure, when lots of other concerns are jostling for our attention. Here's a typical example.

You've been in a job, say, ten years. Recession bites. Unexpectedly you are made redundant and this is very shocking to you. You find yourself doing a round of interviews and having to talk about yourself. Your mood is far from optimistic and your self-esteem has taken a knock. Talking with ease about yourself in this situation, when you haven't practised, will be extremely difficult.

Or consider a situation in which you want to be sexily irresistible: you've just met the man of your dreams. He's everything you're looking for in a life-long partner. He starts to ask you questions about yourself. You're not very good at this. You fumble verbally, sell yourself short, create a Miss Mouse impression while all the time you are desperately thinking: 'What is he thinking about me? Am I making a good impression?'

Now I don't need to tell you that if you've prac-tised talking about yourself and feel confident about it, this situation is much easier to handle. When you're asked about yourself, you answer with comfort. You can focus your attention on the other person, making them comfortable in your company and building a rapport with them. The trouble is, when we haven't been brought up to enjoy talking about ourselves, it can feel like boasting. So in the middle section of this chapter I describe ideas to make boasting comfortable.

An ability to talk well can make people utterly irresistible. And, when good talk is analysed, it always involves the art of story-telling. Compelling communicators like Billy Connolly and Peter Ustinov are irresistible as entertainers because of their skills as raconteurs. Story-telling is a great means of telling others about ourselves, and also a means of entertaining and enlightening others. Following on from the boasting section, then, we investigate story-telling.

Finally, in this chapter we look at probably the most critical context for putting your case forward, and one that a lot of people find very daunting – interviews.

Not so small talk

A couple of years ago, I was keen to write a book on the subject of conversation. On meeting with publishers to discuss it, I was surprised that they regarded this subject as being very down-market, with no appeal whatsoever to professional people. Yet I know from my work that many professionals – lawyers, surgeons and top company executives – welcome insights into how conversation works, and how to improve their skills. For many of these people the demands of making small talk at conferences, for instance, are a secret nightmare.

While some of us are lucky enough to have been brought up to enjoy making conversation, or to have learned to enjoy it, this is certainly not the case for everyone. And there is no correlation between high levels of academic knowledge and professional expertise and the ability to converse. When you think of the extent to which conversation is at the heart of so much of what we do – we get relationships and jobs through it, persuade and influence through it, educate children through it – it's amazing that its workings are a mystery to so many of us.

You'll sometimes hear a person say 'I'm no good at small talk', almost with a sense of pride, as though their minds are preoccupied with much higher things. But small talk performs a very important role in how we interact with one another. It gives us time to judge one another based on the behaviour we observe; it gives us an opportunity to find common ground which we can explore further, and, it gives us the chance to decide whether to progress a relationship further. Through gossip, too, we often learn about what's really going on. Little snippets of information can give us a fuller picture of the complex environments in which the majority of us live and work.

Small talk it may be, but it's of great significance in how we build personal and professional relationships.

How conversation works

Small talk works to a formula. One person makes a statement relating to something that they guess might be common experience. You know, something along the lines of 'Gosh, the traffic's heavy today'. Then they ask a linking question that involves the other person: 'Did you come by car?' With a bit of luck, they'll reply and you will get a conversation going.

When making small talk, you mustn't be too self-critical about the content. When you start to worry about the lack of profundity in your opening, inhibition will strike. Remember – this is Dale Carnegie territory, not Proustian fields. And you may be the sort of person who benefits from thinking beforehand about what you will talk about. I am. In my experience the best sort of spontaneity is always hugely calculated. So, on your way to the event, let your mind wander over interesting news stories, what's happening in your business, any riveting trivia you've heard about recently. Keep these subjects to the front of your brain ready to air.

Good conversation is about being skilled at asking open questions; for example, 'How do you feel about driving?' Rather than the closed 'Do you drive?' It's also about highly receptive and encouraging listening. Nodding, smiling and making *mmn* sounds to indicate your involvement are all part of this. You can't be very cool *and* a good conversationalist. As mentioned in the previous chapter, viewing yourself in the role of researcher again can be very helpful. You want to know what the other person's goals are, what it is they are seeking to do in life, and if you have experiences or knowledge of your own that you can contribute to their ideas.

But you don't have to say a great deal to be a good conversationalist. The art is in asking good open questions, of the 'What do you think?' variety, and then listening in a non-judgemental way. A few years ago, it wasn't considered polite in this country to ask people what they did, early in a conversation. (It's always been regarded as polite in Celtic countries, as are enquiries about income levels . . .) This has changed. But even so, in times of recession, when a lot of people may not be 'doing' anything and rather wish they were, the more diplomatic 'What are you busy with at the moment?' may be better.

Instantly irresistible

- You can start becoming an irresistible conversationalist tomorrow. In a queue, on the bus, in the office canteen, start practising those opening gambits and engaging others in chat.

Gender talk

Socially, and at work, or on other occasions, we can find ourselves trying to be irresistible to members of the opposite sex. So in order to maximise our irresistibility, it seems important to understand how the sexes might take different approaches to conversation.

If you're at all interested in how conversation works, then I can't recommend linguistic professor Deborah Tannen's books highly enough (see Recommended reading on page 324). She gives great insight into how conversation works generally and in *You Just Don't Understand* she examines in detail the different conversational styles of women and men. Whether you want to become more irre-sistible in personal relationships, or professionally, her analysis is invaluable.

When we look at the difference between women and men's conversational aims and styles, it's important to remember that this is generalising. You may be a woman with a very male style, or vice versa. Reading books about the differences between women and men always makes me feel we are like two tribes on different planets, because the central thesis of these books is to emphasise the differences. In real life, optimistic little me suspects there may often be more compromise and under-standing. Nevertheless, while differences in conversation styles may not be completely gender specific, an analysis of difference can help us with that feeling we sometimes get in conversation with someone – that, regardless of their gender, we are on a different planet.

In Deborah Tannen's view, the male planet is one where life is a struggle to maintain independence. The male view of conversation will be that it's an exercise in establishing one's position in a hierarchical social order. They will assume that everyone shares this view of the exercise, and that when a man challenges a woman, she will share this interpretation.

It's just like being on a rugby team. No man would play well as a member of a rugby team if he thought that being aggressive would make him different from the rest of the team. The team norm is that everybody fights and everybody is aggressive and that's OK. You actually show that you're part of the team and acting for the collective good through being aggressive. So it's fine to exercise this aggression on the playing field of conversation. A woman joining an established all-male team at work is likely to find a high level of insulting and teasing – that is all part of this.

On the female planet, life is a struggle to preserve community and connection. Women see themselves as individuals in a network of connections. The female way of maintaining status is by being identified with other people. So women interpret conversation to be about showing similarity and connection, and identification and 'bonding'. It's all about harmony, and conflict will be avoided. Women are more likely to be covert in conversation, concealing disagreement and objections because they don't want to rock the boat. A man joining an all-female team at work may find his co-workers over-interested in his private life and in sharing secrets.

Now I think we can see how women and men might misinterpret one another with these different preoccupations. As Deborah Tannen points out, when a woman sympathises with a man she may well be perceived as being threatening to his sense of independence. He won't see the sympathy as expressing kindness and empathy; he will interpret it as a belittling gesture.

In contrast, as men are so keen on their independence, on striving to maintain this independence, and in getting things sorted out in order to keep being independent, when a woman starts to talk about an emotional problem she's got, or something she's unhappy with – yes, you've guessed it – the chap rushes in to give her a solution. Now this may not be what the woman wants. What she will often want is for the chap to say 'Oh, I'm sorry you feel like that, I can understand how you would', to let her express the problem and to give her a sympathetic response. That's what she would do on the receiving end, after all. But the typical male response is to rush in with a solution resulting in the woman feeling that she's not been heard.

Public and private

The clichéd analysis of the sexes says that women talk far more than men, but, in fact, there is a great deal of research to say that this is not the case. In general, men talk more than women. They also interrupt more and they hold air time for longer. Indeed, one of the ways in which Deborah Tannen says these differences are created is through the public versus private nature of communication between the sexes.

Men, she says, are conditioned to feel comfortable talking in a group in order to establish their status and maintain it. So they get comfortable talking in a public way, and in this contest they are particularly comfortable giving information. Women are much more comfortable talking among friends and equals in a more private context. They are much more comfortable disclosing things about themselves.

This is interesting because when women and men talk in public, different styles will often emerge. Women will tend to use personal examples and experience. Men will find this inappropriate and will be embarrassed by it. Women listening to men may think, 'Yes, well, this is very informative, but it sounds like a lecture. I hear a lot about the principles I should operate under, but I don't hear anything that makes me feel any different.' This response will be created because men tend to think that the purpose of conversation is to give and report information. This, too, is the model of conversation that dominates business.

As a final thought on private and public worlds, I think it's interesting to note the extent to which, in recent years in the Western world, the boundaries between public and private have come crashing down. We live in an age where we know the sex secrets of the so-called great and good: from Mitterrand to Clinton to Prince Charles.

Different ideas about what's effective

Women and men tend to have different ideas about what makes good conversation. A man will view it as being about impersonal matters, factual and task-focused. An example is a meaty conversation about what the England football team should do to win the next world cup. A woman will regard a good conversation as being about personal things. An example is a conversation about sure-fire ways to lose weight, which might involve sharing someone's weight-loss secret. Revealing secrets is a way that women maintain status in conversation, because status comes through association.

Perhaps because of the different ideas women and men hold about the purpose of conversation, different expectations arise about appropriate roles. Because men regard conversation as being about the passing on of information, they are more readily expected to play the expert role. Women, more comfortable in an interactive style, are more readily regarded in the role of nurturers and diplomats, fostering connections. Looking at business and professional conference programmes, and despite the rise of women at work, I find it fascinating to note the extent to which men dominate the public speaking arena. I'd guesstimate that 95 percent of conference speakers are male. Maybe we females don't regard ourselves as experts, or want to push ourselves as such. Or maybe we've just got better things to do with our time.

As a woman who very much wants to be regarded as an expert, or a man who wants to succeed in a nurturing role, sometimes we will need to consider how people's stereotypical expectations may work against us. Flagging them up for people will help clear your listeners' minds of prejudice. Try something like: 'I know it's unusual for you to be listening to a female expert on rear axle suspension' or 'I bet many of you were expecting a female chief nurse here today'.

Instantly irresistible

- When you want to influence the opposite sex through conversation, give them more of what they value. Men should personalise their content for women, and women should remember to give hard information and facts to men.
- This is especially important at the outset of your communication. For several years, I used to speak at medical conferences to largely male groups of surgeons. It took me a while to realise that the audiences became particularly receptive to certain triggers in the openings of these talks. One was a mention of statistics – even though these might have been cited from rather questionable large-scale studies in the social sciences. The other point that seemed to capture their respect was that I'd written books. In their words, that 'I'd published'. Never mind that these were pop psychology books, rather than academic papers. I earned their attention through using triggers that they valued.
- Women need to remember that when men are aggressive in conversation, they may not mean it personally. It's just their interpretation of what's happening. Men need to remember that when women personalise their content, it's because it's highly meaningful, not just an attempt to embarrass them.

Boasting in comfort

As communication becomes increasingly informal, the need to be comfortable talking about yourself becomes more pressing. More and more employers are taking an initially informal approach to re-cruiting, especially in high-tech smallish to medium-sized businesses.

The first encounter you may have with such a firm could be an invitation to 'come over and have a look around'. Your potential direct boss will meet you for a chat and show you around, before inviting you back for a more formal interview. In this context, it may be difficult to know whether you are expected to sell yourself or not. You need to be armed with a direct question, like 'Would you like me to tell you about what I've been doing or shall I save it for another time?' if you sense that you need to seize the moment. Even though this is an apparently informal encounter, you would be wise to prepare material for this opportunity.

When I run workshops and speak at conferences, people sometimes object strongly to me advocating that it's important to become comfortable boasting. They object, I suspect, because they have powerful conditioning that tells them it's inap-propriate, combined with an over-generous view of human beings. They assume, wrongly, that if they go to see someone to chat about a job or some busi-ness, then that person will be very keen to research them and to be predisposed to prise out of them relevant information. In the real world, this is rarely true.

So you need to get comfortable boasting.

And surprise, surprise, women and men have different attitudes towards boasting. Women will often be reluctant to boast because they sense that it will make them unpopular, because they are differentiating themselves from everyone else. Men will regard it as much more acceptable to boast in conversation – after all, that's the way they publicly achieve status when they are with others who are claiming similar status.

In relationships, women will often think men boasted inappropriately at social events. Women are often reluctant to boast about themselves, unless they feel they've been treated unfairly and in their defence bring their achievements to the fore. And again these tendencies will create expectations that may bring censure against people who don't meet them. Take my friend Marian, for example; she has a Ph.D. and was told by her male boss that she was not to use her title at work, as she risked alienating everyone else. We did wonder whether he would have demanded such a thing of a man.

Socially, not many of us in this country enjoy the company of people who boast a great deal. It is very different in the USA, where success is a much more generally accepted value. When we find ourselves boasting a great deal to others, rather than finding out about them, it's usually because we're insecure. And that's the impression others will get. The best way to let people know about your achievements, with some degree of subtlety, is to tell appropriate stories in the form of disclosures, as and when opportunities arise in the flow of conversation.

Accounting for success

How comfortable we are in boasting will depend on how we explain our success. Among highly successful women and men, a far greater number of the women will attribute their success to good fortune and circumstance. The men will be far more inclined to attribute their success to their personal qualities.

But how good we feel about ourselves will also affect these attributions. Here's a reminder about a point I made in Chapter Two. When self-esteem is high, we tend to attribute bad things that happen to outside circumstances and other people. So last week, when you didn't get a promotion, it was the company's fault. When good things happen to us, in this mood, then we explain them through congratulating ourselves personally. When you get an amazing job offer next week, it will be down to your irresistible talents and skills.

As you might expect, when our self-esteem plummets these attributions change. When good things happen, it was pure chance and not down to us personally; when bad things happen, these incidents just endorse even further what a hopeless, lost cause we are. If you are thinking this way, then before you start to practise boasting, you need to boost your self-esteem (see Chapter Two).

Boasting in context

I used to do an exercise in workshops where I asked people to boast about themselves relentlessly for three minutes, during which they were not to make any external attributions. So everything had to be down to them and their amazing abilities. People used to visibly writhe with embarrassment and often run out of content after about a minute. So I stopped being cruel and created an exercise that was much more culturally acceptable, where they put their achievements into a context. Here's an illustration of the contrast in approaches from a web-site designer:

> I started my business five years ago. I worked very hard and made some inspired decisions about the marketing. I very quickly built up some long-term relationships which have been extremely rewarding.

Listening to that, many of us would be tempted to put our fingers down our throats and to say '*yuck*' . . .

In contrast:

> I started my business five years ago, when people were getting very interested in the internet. I tried

to be creative about the marketing, worked hard, and discovered there was a vast amount of available business. The timing and growth in my sector helped me build some long-term relationships, which have been extremely rewarding.

Slightly more long-winded, perhaps, but to my ears and, I hope, yours, much more palatable.

When we put things into context, we describe the big picture. Social, economic, political and technological trends can all be relevant. Your own family background may feature. Slightly tangential details may add colour and memorability. The ability to see the big picture is a prized one today, especially with the speed of change in the environments in which most of us live and work. So to use this ability when we talk about ourselves serves two purposes – it makes us feel more comfortable boasting and it shows a broad mind. 'Big picture' thinking is often described as a desirable attribute of leaders.

So rather than: 'When I won my scholarship to Oxford', go for: 'I got a scholarship to Oxford, which was great for my family because I was the first person to go to university'. Rather than: 'I was top saleswoman of the year for seven years running and the company's top performer', go for: 'For seven years – and they were great years because the economy was so healthy – I was top saleswoman of the year and also the company's top performer'. Rather than: 'I have a second home, a country cottage in Devon', go for: 'When we won the law case, we blew it all on our country cottage in Devon'. It's much more human and appealing.

In truth, too, much of what happens to us is a combination of factors in our environment and our own qualities. Like my favourite definition of luck – which can be described as the combination of preparation and opportunity.

Funny old you

Another way to become comfortable boasting is to use humour. Now humour always involves a target, and as Freud pointed out, it is often aggressive. This is why it is almost impossible to be funny and politically correct, because very often the target of humour is people who are vulnerable, or outside the norm in some way. That's why jokes about the Welsh are funny.

Now, of course, I can say that as a Welsh person, because I'm directing the comment against myself. Self-effacing humour works well because you direct the humour against yourself – in the knowledge that you are a safe target, and no one will be offended. The only proviso to be made here is that in some highly formal situations, using humour, even against oneself, may be regarded as flippancy, and a sign that you are not taking the situation seriously enough.

Much of the time, though, humour is a great ice-breaker and leveller. It happens through leaps of connection between parts of the brain, which are always unexpected. So in my next paragraph, I'm going to tell you how to fart irresistibly.

OK, so that comment was somewhat school-boyish in tone and not that funny, but it makes the point. If you smiled, however wanly, it was because the comment was unexpected and smutty.

Self-effacing humour shows great confidence. It's also a good way of dealing with prejudices that people may hold against you. Like the accountant who introduces herself with: 'Hello, I'm Helen the accountant and to try and allay any fears you might have that accountants are boring, I'm going to speak for only five minutes at this meeting and try and make it as stimulating as possible.'

We can use self-effacing humour to boast in a way that people will find endearing. I'm secretly very proud of the fact that in the past I've been hired to give advice to a conservative prime minister and worked on the Labour Party election campaign, but I find people enjoy finding out about it much more if I describe these jobs as 'discredits' on my cv, and imply, jokingly, that I'm rather ashamed of them.

Humour directed at oneself indicates a great deal of self-acceptance and self-confidence; these are irresistible qualities. Dawn French, Clive James and Tony Blair quite clearly do care about what other people think about themselves, but are able to go beyond this, to joke about themselves, and ideas and prejudices others may have about them. You can't take yourself too seriously. It's always a sign of insecurity that you're worrying that others won't take you to be so.

The self-effacing use of humour is a shrewd device to endear people towards you because you're not precious or earnest about yourself, and a device that subtly indicates how really confident you are.

Let's now look at another way of getting comfortable talking about ourselves.

Story-telling

Stories are our most powerful form of communication. We make sense of everything that has happened to us through stories and they give us our sense of identity. We use them to structure time and memories. In stories, our needs for pattern and resolution are satisfied.

All of us have heard stories since we were very small. The form is so familiar to us that we become especially receptive when we hear a speaker start to tell a story.

A few months ago, I attended a workshop run by a therapist called Pat Williams, which was all about story-telling in therapy. Her stories about results with clients, using story-telling to help them over-come seemingly insuperable problems, were very inspiring. She told us an especially moving story about a boy with severe psychiatric problems who would not come out of his room. Pat sat at the top of the stairs telling him story after story of kings shut in castles, and wise women in towers and young princes on islands. Eventually, after many hours, the door opened slightly and a little face peered out to make contact with his story-teller. While Pat was exhausted, the poor parents were ecstatic at the development.

When we're comfortable telling stories about ourselves, we have at our disposal a means of letting people know something about us, in all sorts of contexts. Just meeting somebody over dinner, or chatting to someone in a wine bar, or that situation I described earlier where a potential employer or supplier asks you along for a chat – in all these instances, the ability to tell stories about yourself is invaluable.

You will already have many stories in your head that explain how you came to be where you are today. I have some – the one about me being the first person in my family to go to university, the one about coming to London believing that the pavements were paved with gold, the one about the very lucky period I went through when I started my own business. You might find it helpful to pause for a moment to think about your favourite stories about your life.

How do stories work? Well they have to have beginnings, middles and ends. There is no set formula for effective story-telling, but stories often have certain features. There's usually an incident that starts the story off: 'I was turned down for my fifth job interview, so I decided to do something about it.'

There may well be complications: 'The trouble was, as I'd not been working for a while, I didn't have much money.'

Things may well turn into a crisis: 'What was I going to do? I was desperate for a job, but I felt so low and worthless, I didn't think I had a chance of getting one.'

Then there's often a climax, involving a change of fortune: 'A friend suggested I embarked on a low-cost irresistibility campaign . . . and lent me this book.'

Finally, the resolution: 'I put lots of the advice into practice and two months later got the job of my dreams.'

Stories don't necessarily need all of these features, but they will always have some of them, and they always need a resolution. You'll almost certainly have come across someone who tells stories that don't resolve. It's always rather embarrassing to listen to these, as nobody knows when the story has ended and where they should respond. Sometimes, too, stories fail because the teller doesn't build a sense of crisis enough. This is the area that builds the tension and makes us think 'My goodness, this is a bit of a cliff-hanger'. This makes story-listening exciting as we wait for the climax and resolution.

Clients have told me that they find this story-telling exercise extremely effective. I have used it with people who find it extremely difficult to talk about themselves, and watched them transform into animated and enthusiastic self-publicists. For people preparing to sell themselves in the work-place and others who want to be more entertaining and comfortable socially, this formula seems to work very well.

Mystical powers

Pat Williams, who I mentioned earlier and who runs story-telling workshops, suggests that when we are facing difficult problems, creating meta-phors in the shape of stories can be extremely helpful. Something to do with bringing the un-conscious into action on the conscious, I suspect. Here's an experience of this:

A few years ago, I was working on a book and, as usual, halfway through I became hugely worried about whether I had enough content. I decided to relax on the sofa and see if a story came to mind that might help. This was what occurred:

A princess lived in a tower and she had a large treasure chest which was half-full of gold coins. She was very concerned to fill up the treasure chest. She asked her courtiers to help her do this. 'But Princess,' they said, 'what do you want this treasure for?'

'To give to the people in the village,' she replied.

'Then Princess,' they said, 'we will need to carry the chest down to the village, for the people to help themselves to the treasure. As it is now, we can manage that. If it gets much heavier, we cannot.'

'Then take it,' she said. And the people came and helped themselves to the treasure.

And that book, which was light and accessible, is still travelling well out of the bookshops, even today.

Instantly irresistible

- Practise telling stories about yourself, talk them aloud into a tape recorder or a video camera so that you get used to hearing them, and play them back and think how they could be improved and where there could be more or less detail.
- As a parent with small children, listen to the stories you tell, bearing in mind the features that I've described here. You'll soon hear most stories have these features. Newspaper stories have these features, too. Listen to good raconteurs and how they use these features.
- Read books of short stories to familiarise yourself with the form.
- What roles do you play in your favourite stories about your life? Can you retell the stories where you are passive and a victim of circumstance as ones where you are a heroine or hero?

Before we go on to talk about interviews, a quick hark back to an earlier theme in this chapter. Left to their own invention, women and men take different approaches to story-telling. Men tend to tell stories about themselves, featuring themselves as central characters. They will often act alone in their stories, and their themes are usually to do with overcoming opposition and obstacles. You know the sort of thing – overpowering killer whales, hunting for gorgons, or fighting off a hostile bid from some venture capitalists.

Women's stories tend to describe incidents that happen to others, to feature community and action from groups of people. Their stories will often involve some violation of social norms, either by themselves or other people. Rather than overcoming difficulties, they are likely to feature themselves helping others. You know the sort of thing, going out of the house, having forgotten to put a skirt on, helping someone who's had an accident, or how a group of friends got together to form a reading group.

Interviews

The idea of interviews strikes terror in the hearts of many people, especially if they haven't been for an interview for years. We sense that we're being judged during an interview and so we perform a psychological phenomenon called projection, where we assume that the people in the interview are thinking as critically about us as we are of ourselves. So if we feel that we are somewhat inarticulate, or a little bit vague, or quiet, or waffley, then we will immediately assume that is what the interviewers are thinking of us. But, of course, this is not always so.

It's worth remembering before any interview that the interviewers themselves are possibly under pressure. Their job performance may be measured quite severely by how well they recruit and they may be seeing a lot of people in rather stressed conditions. Certainly, in the large companies where I've observed recruitment, there's been last-minute panic before the interviews start, with a great palaver about room allocations, missing c.v.s and alterations to the schedule.

It's most important, too, to remember that when we prepare for an interview, we are often using a distinct set of skills from those we use in our jobs. The skills of selling yourself during an interview may be far removed from your day-to-day work, especially if your role involves a high degree of technical expertise, with little people interaction. While interviewing would be an excellent method of recruiting, say, a politician – whose job involves going on television and radio a lot to answer difficult questions – its suitability is questionable for a role where communication skills are of little importance.

Interviewing isn't a very scientific way of choosing people for jobs, despite the best efforts of many organisations to make it as bias-free as possible. Human beings find it impossible to be utterly objective about one another. I know that when I've observed 'objective' interviewing, where every word that the interviewee says is transcribed, bias still prevails. When the transcription is reviewed as to how well it fits with the carefully chosen selection criteria, bias occurs in what's chosen as evidence from the transcription. Interviewers take a shine to people who remind them of themselves, and give greater precedence to desirable content in their answers.

Many interviewers have a bias towards recruiting in their own image. And it's very difficult to eliminate this. I suspect that the real reason businesses persist in using such a method for recruitment is to do with the 'people like us' factor. Any of you who visit lots of different businesses like I do will know that there are very clearly Marks & Spencer types of people, Hewlett Packard types of people and Goldman Sachs types of people. Organisations attract a certain type of person and through interviewing they will recruit more of that type of people. So that's why interviewing remains popular. While attracting similar types of people may be bad for organisations, in that perspectives are limited, it probably cuts down on in-fighting. More of employees' energy can go into profiting the business than contending with Denzil from supplies, 'who doesn't seem to understand what the company's about'. Attracting similar types of people, however, may mean that those people become smug and complacent through constant reinforcement of their self-image. They may lose essential contact with the world outside the company and its markets.

You're probably best off accepting that interviewing demands a certain set of skills, and it's worth honing those skills for when you need them.

Getting ready for interviews

I've come across people who dread interviews so much that they don't do any preparation for them whatsoever. Very unwise ostriches. There's a great deal you can do beforehand to give yourselves a competitive edge.

Start with you. It's a good idea to look at your c.v. and career history as a story. What have been the turning points, highs and lows, complications and crises that have shaped this story? Very probably, there may be several stories there: person hell-bent on self-development and achievement striving against the odds, for example, or person struggling to balance personal and professional demands, or even person being given incredibly lucky break, as another example.

If these stories aren't featuring you as the heroine or hero, but a victim of circumstance, then they need rewriting in your head. You need to become victor over circumstance. Using the story formula I gave you earlier, you could shape these stories into useful chatty content – for meetings or interviews.

Your achievement inventory

Next, you need to create an inventory of your achievements. People get very blinkered here, usually from a sense of panic that says, 'I've done nothing with my life.' Here are some questions you could ask yourself to identify a wide range of your achievements. Have I:

- organised matters?
- made things more efficient?
- saved or made money?
- solved problems?
- spoken or written particularly effectively?
- taken risks that have paid off?
- run a team well?
- been a good team player?
- motivated myself and others?
- been very flexible?
- been original and creative?
- coached and counselled others?
- given 'added value' and 'gone the extra mile'?

It's worth taking a few days to mull over your history and to come up with every possible achievement, and then to shape them into nifty little formulae of assignment/action/achievement.

Assignment means describing the initial situation and this needs to be description in broad strokes. So it's:

'A new chief executive joined the company who

wanted to radically change our department,'

rather than:

'In May 1997, a new chief executive Roger Thomas joined the company and one of his top priorities was to change the way our department in particular worked, so he organised a review and what they found was . . .'

by the end of which an interviewer will be snoozing.

Action means what you did. I would use a maximum of three verbs. Again, I'll illustrate:

'So I told everyone what was happening, reassured them their jobs were safe and got them trained on the new system.'

This is much punchier than:

'Well, I was a bit nervous about telling everyone but I did anyway and then some of them were a bit worried about their jobs, so I sought reassurance from Roger that . . .'

And, finally, the really important bit of the formula, your: **Achievement**, needs to be as specific and quantifiable as it can be. So it's:

'In six months, everyone was really happy using the new system and we had a 35 percent increase in productivity,'

rather than:

'People were a lot happier after the training and they quite soon got to like the new system and Roger was pleased, too, because our department did seem to be that much more effective.'

The number of these **AAA**s you can come up

with will depend on how long your career has been. I'd say roughly that you should be able to aim to get three of them for every five years you've been working. You could, of course, choose to cite achievements from outside the workplace, and these might include any sort of changes which you've handled well (having kids, taking a sabbatical, being made redundant, coping with illness, etc.)

These AAAs provide you with rock-solid content, and very specific examples with which to sell yourself. It's worth writing them down and commiting them to memory, and storing them right in the front of your mind. There, they can act as a carousel of examples from which you can pull relevant ones, depending on the interview question. I'd regard this as the core act of preparing for interviews.

Once you're sorted out, you need to investigate your potential employer.

Research, research, research

This is largely a matter of common sense, but it's amazing how that can fly out of the window when people are panicking. It's just a matter of finding out everything you can about your potential employer, in national and trade press, libraries, on the internet and through talking to people. Lurk around outside at opening and closing times, if you want to get a feel for the people there and how they present themselves.

Find out all you can about the job on offer and the interview – who'll be there, is there a follow-up, is there any specific preparation they would like you to do? Remember, though, that quite often people interview without a clear idea of who they're looking for, and they are waiting for you to make an entrance saying, 'I'm the one.'

Practise, practise, practise

Rehearse for your interview aloud. After all, that is the medium for which you are preparing. By all means have your AAAs down on paper and perhaps some other ideas, but remember that you are speaking this content, not preparing it to be read. Use friends, work colleagues, tape and video recorders to give you feedback.

Self-effacing people often have trouble with the 'I' word, so it's especially important to get used to hearing yourself saying that. Use 'I' when you mean you, 'we' when you mean everyone in your company, team or the world. Don't use 'one'. Who does it mean?

Prepare answers to all those horrible clichéd questions like, 'Where do you see yourself in five years' time?' and 'What are your strengths and weaknesses?' The tactic here is to describe a weakness that would be rather irrelevant to the role. And remember, too, as I mentioned earlier, that all weaknesses, with a slight shift of interpretation, can be seen as strengths. Impatience can become decisiveness, slow-thinking can become contemplative, and ruthless can become extremely focused.

If there are holes in your c.v. where you didn't work, then prepare positive content to show how you used that time profitably. Those five years in Wormwood Scrubs become the period when you got the equivalent of a Ph.D. in basket-weaving.

Get your clothes and appearance sorted out a couple of days beforehand. A good haircut can do wonders for most of us. You don't want to find the baby's been sick on the shoulder of your black jacket on the morning of the interview. If you're taking anything along to the interview, such as tangible evidence of previous achievements, get that ready, too.

When you feel nervous before an interview, don't worry, because adrenalin will sharpen your performance. Warm yourself up physically, use your voice a bit beforehand, warming up those facial muscles, and check your breathing is slow and controlled. As you walk into the room keep using the actioning technique to tell yourself what it is you are doing. You know, 'I'm walking across the floor; I'm looking at the interviewers; I'm shaking their hands.' Have a clear idea about what your intentions are during the interview – perhaps you will be enthusing, reassuring, convincing or selling, for instance.

During the interview

Avoid paranoia. OK, it goes to some people's heads when they're put in the role of an interviewer and they start to act like Pol Pot. If that's the case you probably don't want to work for them or possibly even the company. When we get paranoid we start to think there must be right or wrong answers to every question. This is not necessarily so.

The other day I met someone who'd been a member of a government security service. They told me that potential officers would be asked the gob-smacking interview question: 'What's your mental age and how do you account for it?' Many candidates thought there must be a 'right' answer to this. But, of course, there wasn't. The question was designed to get candidates to demonstrate self-knowledge. A mental age of three could be a satisfactory answer, where the candidate gave a good account of why they'd chosen that age. Mind you, I suppose if you're thinking of joining the security services a healthy dose of paranoia may not be such a bad thing . . .

In most instances, what interviewers are seeking is a match between role requirements and you as candidate. Be as specific as possible in your answers. The most common tendency of poor interview technique is to waffle on in the abstract. So when you are asked a question like, 'What do you think makes a great manager?' it's not a great idea to rabbit on about your opinions of the latest research to come out of Harvard. Much better to name a quality, for instance, 'good communication skills', and then to give one of your AAAs as tangible evidence of when you personally demonstrated this.

Interviewees often panic when presented with a 'What would you do if?' question for which they have not prepared. In this instance, you can either describe the general principles and priorities you would use, and/or cite a specific and similar instance in the past, and describe what you did then.

In any doubt about what to do in an interview, then ask. Where to sit, whether the interviewer would like you to expand upon an answer, what a question means, if you're not clear. Much better to do this than to make assumptions and get it wrong.

You can sell yourself on three levels. You can offer reasons to people, much of which will be in your c.v. But, then, don't assume they've read it. You can sell yourself at an emotional level, where you reassure the interviewers and motivate them. And you can sell yourself at an imaginative level, where they see you doing the role in the future, from your description of, and level of engagement with, what you've done in the past.

Instantly irresistible

- Your uniqueness will increase your irresistibility to interviewers. Emphasise this through odd combinations of skills and interests you might have.

- Positive elements are much more irresistible than negative ones. Uplifting emotions like enthusiasm are highly contagious. So if you want them to be enthusiastic about you, convey enthusiasm yourself. When you plan your content, find every opportunity to demonstrate what you really care about, and what your top values and priorities are.
- Plan to do something really enjoyable after your interview. It'll help you keep a sense of perspective and stay more relaxed.

So there you go, m'luds – lots of ideas to make talking about yourself easier. It's down to you, now. You'll make a great start on your irresistibility if you just put one of these ideas into practice in the next twenty-four hours. I dare you to go and have a great conversation with somebody. Who knows what might happen afterwards.

6

Deciding about You

Your Calvin Kleins or your DKNYs for today? What about the job offer – should you take it? Toast or fruit for breakfast? Should you suggest cohabitation to your lover? Are you going to the gym later?

Modern life is full of decision-taking, and the more we know about the process, the better decisions we will take. A vital element of irresistibility is knowing as much as possible about how people are taking decisions about you. Why will people decide that you should be given a job rather than anybody else? What will affect the board's decision to give your pet project their financial go-ahead? Will certain factors determine whether your lover says 'yay' or 'nay' to your proposal?

In Chapter Three we discussed concrete laws that determine how people influence others to take decisions; in this chapter we analyse every aspect of decision-taking with great thoroughness. As well as giving you insight into how others decide, this chapter will also help you to make the best possible decisions for yourself.

One of the fantasies we often hold about taking decisions is that there must be a single, best, fail-safe way of taking them. But this is not the case. Different decisions will have different goals behind them. It all depends on what we want to achieve.

Let's take a mundane everyday decision that one person, called Miranda, might take: how to get to work in the morning. Miranda might have two different goals she considers about this decision. Does she want her journey to work to be efficient, which she defines as using the minimum amount of energy, or does she want her journey to be effective, which she defines as getting the best results. If she plumps for efficient, she might imagine she'll jump on the tube line, get a seat if she's lucky and get to work with the minimum expenditure of energy, but some cash outlay.

But as the tube service has a reputation for being unreliable, Miranda might be wiser using effectiveness as the goal of her decision. She could decide to walk to work. She'll use up more energy and get fitter, but more importantly, while her journey will take longer, she's almost certainly guaranteed to get there.

Another pet idea that people have about decision-taking is that it should be either a logical process or an intuitive one. That we should either use reasoning and pros and cons, or use gut reaction. But in our minds both these reactions occur at the same time. It's unwise to rely exclusively on either approach, even though we may have a preference for one over the other.

So, in this chapter I look at how we make solo decisions, how groups decide, and some exercises and ideas we can use to improve our own decision-making. By the end of this chapter, you will have a great deal of information and insight into how you can get decisions made in your favour.

Solo decisions

Here are some guidelines about influences on people who are taking individual decisions about you.

We see what we want or expect to

My two-year-old and four-year-old boys love playing outside in the garden. Every morning I go into their bedroom, draw back the curtains and we discuss the weather. As we're in Britain, my comments are usually about grey skies, clouds, and glimmers of possibility of sunshine. In contrast, my four-year-old makes comments about sunshine, blue skies and it being a great day to go out and play in the garden. That's what he wants to see and wants me to see, too.

The way in which we receive information is highly selective. Our brains, without us consciously being aware of it, will scan for information that is relevant to us. What's relevant will depend on our past experiences, our background, personality and preferences. And, of course, what we value and want in life.

An antique dealer, a frequent hostess and a soap opera fan will all see the same room very differently. The dealer will spot the Queen Anne chair in the corner; the hostess, the large round table, perfect for dinner parties; and the soap opera fan will notice the 24-inch screen television and remember that it's almost time for *EastEnders*. Our brains will screen information unconsciously before we identify, sort and make sense of it. Through feedback loops our memories will filter what we receive before our conscious thinking is aware of it. For our brains simply could not cope with taking in all the sensory data that surrounds us. The attention span required would be too great.

It's the same with listening. In a crowded party, you will almost certainly not attend to the person in your group with the loudest voice if you hear a speaker in the group next to yours mention your name several times. The temptation to eavesdrop on a conversation in which you feature will be much too compelling.

Our old friends, the estate agents, make use of

clients having selective attention. Showing you round a property, a shrewd estate agent will draw your attention immediately to what they consider to be the best features. You go into a drawing room and the agent immediately draws your attention to the stunning marble fireplace. They'll wax lyrical about it, in order to prevent your attention wandering to the cracked wall behind the sofa, opposite. They'll want that visual feast to figure high in your decision-making criteria.

We see what we want to in order to confirm our beliefs and our loyalties. At the time of writing, Wales has just beaten England at rugby, scoring dramatically in the last ten minutes. In recent years this has been a rare event, so please allow me to crow here. We Welsh supporters and the Welsh press regard this victory as exciting evidence of the revival of Welsh rugby. But our English friends seem to regard it as something completely different. They see it as something to do with a critical refereeing decision in the last ten minutes.

Instantly irresistible

- When people are taking important decisions about you, it's worth thinking about any expectations and beliefs they may be bringing to the situation, and researching these where possible. Also, when you're making important decisions about your future, you'll find it helpful to consult with people who don't necessarily share your expectations and beliefs. This will help free your decision of bias.

- Give people who are making decisions about you obvious confirming evidence of your best attributes. Going for a top manager's job, they need to get an overwhelming sense, through how you look and act, that you are familiar and comfortable in this role – whether you are, or not. The same directive applies to your c.v. This should be jiggled around depending on what you want to highlight, with the most relevant information very near the top. Abandon a chronological account of your achievements where the relevant information is buried deep in what you were doing five years ago.

We act to close the gap between belief and behaviour

This idea comes from a grandly titled psychological theory: 'Festinger's Theory of Cognitive Dissonance.' Not one to try if your teeth are loose. What this boils down to is that we act to close the gap between what we believe and our behaviour. It's a principle that's vital in some of the laws of irresistibility I mentioned in Chapter Three: the laws of consistency and scarcity.

Just to remind you, the law of consistency says

that, by and large, we like to view ourselves as being consistent. So, if your boss has a strong sense of morality as part of her self-image, but comes up with the suggestion of investing in tobacco shares, then reminding her of your view of her as a principled individual could prevent her folly. Her decision will be based on her desire to close the gap between her belief – in this instance her self-image – and what she does.

When you've retired and taken up antique-collecting and fancy an antique vase, which the dealer tells you is in rare supply, then the law of scarcity will be influencing you. You will believe it to be more valuable, because of its scarcity, and act to close the gap between what you believe and your behaviour – in other words, the desire to buy it. So you'll act to close the gap between belief and behaviour, by parting with a small fortune.

When people are making decisions about you, then, the more they believe that you are special and in demand, the better. Your early presentation to them needs to show them that you value yourself and are valuable to others. What you categorically do not want to do is to create the impression that you are desperate or will do anything to get a gig. Market realities may make you feel like this, but you mustn't let it show. Remember, too, that when you meet people who may be involved in making decisions about you in the future, a good first impression will encourage them to keep their behaviour in line with beliefs they will have formed about you earlier. You are more likely to get a positive result from them.

Instantly irresistible

- Create the belief in someone powerful that you are worth nurturing, and they may act to close the gap between their belief and your actuality. If you've to attend a meeting with a senior manager, then ask beforehand to be briefed about the role they'd like you to play. If you're trying to improve your meeting performance in any way, ask them for specific comments afterwards. And following the meeting, ask for feedback. This will show them you are enthusiastic and engage their interest in your performance. Very useful when, six months later, your promotion review comes up in discussion.

  People don't do this nearly enough. It's not being creepy – there's a fair exchange going on. The senior person feels flattered to have their wisdom invited, and the junior person receives patronage.

- Effectiveness of the free trial as a tactic needn't be confined to Pampers nappies coming through your letter-box, or *Reader's Digest* subscriptions. When you're trying to get someone to follow a course of action, or buy a service, getting them to sample the proposal in some pleasurable way will encourage them to close the gap between what they believe and what they're prepared to do.

Our memories select and distort

'*You must remember this, a kiss is just a kiss, a sigh is just a sigh*' goes that old *Casablanca* song. But was it 'just a kiss' to both of them? Couldn't it have been much more significant to one of them than the other?

The point here is that to some extent, we make up our memories. They may originate in truth but we add our own personal details and selective perception. Many of us have an image of memory as a storage house, where events are parcelled up, available for us to unwrap when we wish. But it doesn't really work like that.

To experience what I mean, choose one of your fondest memories and give it a mental replay. Go for a really good one – with you in a Mae West or Robert Redford role. I bet, in most cases, you will have put yourself as a character in that memory. You will play a role in it; you will see yourself in scenes in that memory. It's as though you're watching a film of the past, while being outside yourself. But, of course, that was not how you experienced what happened; you experienced events while being completely within them. Your memory has shifted perspective on them and it can't work any other way. We can't actually go back to what happened, even though some of us may think our memories work like that.

You'll have had experience of this, I'm sure, when listening to a relative or a friend describing an event where you were present. Your recollection may be completely different from theirs. Now I've a very good friend who remembers many things we've experienced together as examples of catastrophe: medical tests, dramas involving the police, accidents. Rack my memory banks as much as I can – and I can sometimes recall the incidents – I never remember her dramatic catastrophic versions of them.

And spin doctors use this guideline to rewrite history. We are reminded constantly that the previous government were a bad lot, by whatever government is in power. So that whether we thought so at the time, or not, the overwhelming impression is created of a series of events which were all indicative of bad government.

Often, too, in couples, one person may describe something the couple have experienced, leaving their partner blinking with disbelief at the dramatisation of events. Does this sound familiar?

One of the tricks memory plays on us is to give us hindsight bias, or 'I knew it all along' thinking. Our memories will recreate a far greater sense of conviction that something was going to happen than we actually felt at the time. Our decisions will be affected then through this sort of thinking: 'I bought retail shares five years ago and I knew all along they were going to do well and they have.' This is an example of hindsight bias because we didn't really know they were going to do well. When we decide to buy more retail shares on the basis of this imaginary 'I knew it all along' idea, we could be getting into trouble.

Hindsight bias is all part of the way we human beings desire to look and feel good. To think that we have predicted the future accurately makes us seem smart – to ourselves and others.

When people are making decisions about us, the more we know about them, their history and how that may connect with us, the better. Gossiping to other people and listening intently is a good way of getting information about decision-makers. The more we can confirm for the decision-taker that their approval of us is the right line, the more they can savour the prospect of saying, 'I knew all along she was the right manager to give the funding to.'

When describing your history or how you currently spend your time, it is your interpretation of what's significant that we hear. There is always an element of 'spinning', in that you prioritise the details you give people about your past or your present. It's canny to attach that significance in the direction of the opportunity you're seeking. To expand what I mean, here's Simon's experience:

> I'm a graphic designer and I do three different things: write for a design magazine occasionally, produce brochures for corporate clients and produce what I would regard as graphic art. Sometimes, when I go to pitch for corporate work, I know I sound like someone who spends most of their time producing corporate brochures, rather than the maximum of three days a week which I

choose to do. I don't think this is disingenuous – it's just that the people I'm pitching to will have brochure design as their absolute top priority, and want to hire consultants who share this priority. If I were to give much mention to my other activities, they might use this as a criteria for not choosing me – that I'm a dabbler, rather than a focused professional. Even though I've an impressive ten-year track record, I still think it's worth taking this precaution.

Instantly irresistible

- When you are trying to persuade somebody to do something that they are resisting because they've had a bad experience when they tried it before, get them to replay the attempt and to talk about how they might have achieved a good outcome, and how this would have felt. This might break down the resistance they are feeling, based on hindsight bias.

- Similarly, to reduce your own tendencies to hindsight bias – 'I did it this way before and it worked out incredibly well, just like I thought it would' – replay the scenario with a very different outcome and things going badly wrong. Then, take your decision.

- A person's history is open to many interpretations. Where the legal system permits it, defence lawyers may use a reframing device, called 'stealing thunder'. Here's an example:

The defendant, Bill Sykes, is in the dock for theft. The lawyer for his defence describes him thus: 'And, yes, the defendant Bill Sykes has committed theft twice before. This was over five years ago, and since then he has accepted his punishment and, through extensive counselling, become a new man. He now works as a highly thought-of stockbroker and spends much of his leisure time doing charity work. Certainly, he is not now the kind of man who would commit theft. No one would believe that of him.'

The defence lawyer here has defined the significance of Bill's past and made his misdeeds sound much less important than if the prosecution lawyer had been allowed the opportunity to describe them first. The defender has stolen the prosecutor's thunder.

We experience everything in its context

This means that when people make decisions about you, they will be affected by where you met and who they met before and after you, and with whom you associate.

This is an expansion of the ideas mentioned in Chapter Three, when we talked about the law of comparison – which says that everything we experience is in relation to something else. If I asked you to pour yourself three beakers of water – one very hot, one tepid and one cold – and you tasted the very hot one followed by the tepid one, it would be a different experience than if you tasted the cold one, then the tepid one. And if you're obsessive enough to go try this, be careful.

Generally speaking, this influence of context means that we are very influenced by the first presentation we receive of something: be it the cover of a book, a receptionist at a company's HQ, or a beautifully presented hors d'oeuvre in a restaurant. Clever salespeople will aim to make a very favourable first impression, because they know this generates a halo effect. In other words, if we give a person or a thing one good attribute, then we assume that other good attributes will follow.

Psychology studies in the 1920s showed that if a teacher was judged to have very good teaching skills, they were also regarded as having a better appearance, to be healthier, to be better at time-keeping, to be more intellectual and to have more integrity and sincerity than teachers who were judged less able at teaching. The experiments also showed that if people liked a teacher's voice, they would also judge the teacher to be more intelligent and more interested in community affairs than a teacher who didn't have such a pleasant voice.

We are generally highly irrational about how we use the halo effect. Politicians and celebrities exploit this to the full by banging on endlessly about the good things they've done, so that we associate other good qualities with the quality about which they are being so 'in-our-faces'.

Another critical aspect about the context of decision-making is timing. If people are making a decision quickly, they are likely to be influenced by what's called 'primacy effect'. We will be influenced to favour what we experience first. Let's say you decide you want to buy a new car and go out one Saturday afternoon to a car showroom, keen to make a decision. A canny salesperson may show you two cars – one at £15,000 and one at £10,000. In that order, of course. They'll suggest you generate a 'for and against' list for the first car and then the second. The probability is that your choice will be the first car, because of primacy effect.

When a comparison is separated by time, however, something called the 'recency effect' comes into play, which says that we are influenced more by what we experienced last. So if you are going to pitch for business against competition and you know they are seeing several contenders over a period of, say, three weeks, you would be better off making your pitch towards the end of the three-week period and, if you can, going last. You will be remembered best and the recency effect will work to your advantage.

The order in which we receive information influences our decision-taking. Ashe, a famous social psychologist, described two different people using the following lists:

a. intelligent, kind, envious, impulsive
b. envious, impulsive, intelligent, kind

Even though there were no stated implications about the degree of these qualities, the a-list people were regarded as a better bunch than the b-list people, just because the favourable adjectives were up front.

Instantly irresistible

- When offering people options about the course of action they would like to take, it's often wisest to give them three alternatives. If you just offer them two, clever people will invent a third.
- It's also wise to put the course of action you would like them to take *last*. They are less likely to think that you're pushing this option. It's the difference between: 'Do you want to let me know now or do you want to write or to fax me?' and 'Do you want to write or to fax me, or let me know now?'
- Presenting an argument, get your most important point in early to grab 'em. If you don't know how long their decision will take and whether they're hearing other cases, then guarantee using the recency effect by repeating this point at the end.

We are never completely objective

However apparently rational someone taking a decision about you is, they can never be completely objective. The fact that you don't speak French, which is a stated requisite of the role, may be ignored by them, because they were so fired up by your enthusiasm and customer focus.

For the lovers of reason among us, it would be marvellous in decision-taking if we could simply take all the possible alternatives, study them and weigh up the consequences in detail, before making our choice. Practically, and in reality, we very rarely have time to do this. And even if we were able, time-wise, to do this, our memory of courses of action we had taken in the past would be likely to determine the alternatives we selected.

Take the example of looking for a property. If you're looking for a flat and aiming to do it really objectively, then you should probably see several hundred flats that fit your criteria, over a period of about six months. But nobody in their right mind would do this – though I do know a fusspot or two who've got pretty close. What we look for is something that satisfies enough of our needs – what the research psychologist Herbert Simon described as 'satisfycing' ourselves with as word invented, rather than optimising the decision. We don't run an exhaustively objective search of everything that's available. Were we to do that, we would never know when to stop.

Whenever we persuade anybody else to do something, we are presenting them with our tour around the evidence. We can never be sure that we have all the evidence and information available.

Let's say you're an expert on the Big Mac burger. Yes, I know it's an odd thing to be, but someone has to do it. You know millions of facts about the Big Mac. You are on your way to lecture me on the properties of the Big Mac. As your student, I discover a new fact about the Big Mac, during your journey. If you're hung up on a definition of yourself as this Mac-expert, and threatened by other people knowing about it, then when you arrive and I present you with this newly discovered fact, you will feel undermined. But there's nothing you can do about this, only change your attitude. As experts, we can only be confident that we know where to find the latest facts.

Instantly irresistible

- If you are someone who loves detailed analysis, thoroughness and collecting data, you may, at times, find these features hamper you in your decision-making. You may overlook the impossibility of having all the facts and detail at your fingertips. You may get bogged down by detail and make your decisions too late. You'll be better off giving yourself strict time deadlines by which to take decisions, and then researching what's most important to know by that time. Then you'll need to leap in and make the decision whether you feel ready or not.

We are affected by language

Your use of words will affect your decision-taker. 'I quite enjoyed working there' will not be as powerful as 'I really loved working there'. Words affect how people take decisions. A group of students was shown film of a car crash and asked to estimate how fast the car was travelling when it *contacted* the other car. Another group of students was shown the same film, and asked to estimate how fast the car was travelling when it *smashed* the other car. The second group, receiving that much more theatrical use of language, estimated a considerably higher speed.

The words we use put a spin on things. A 1986 British Gallup Poll asked people whether 'Britain's nuclear weapons make you feel *safe*?' Forty percent replied 'yes'. When people were asked whether 'Britain's nuclear weapons made them feel *safer*?' 50 percent replied 'yes'. We mild Brits obviously feel happier committing ourselves to the comparative state of safer, rather than a categorical one of safe or unsafe.

We can load language, too, to make it sound more socially desirable. Fewer people will say 'yes' to: 'Should our country give shelter to refugees from the Balkans? – ethnically cleansed by the dictator Milosovic?' And more people are likely to say 'yes' to: 'Should we not allow refugees in this country?' than are likely to give an affirmative response to the question: 'Should we forbid refugees to come into this country?' That's because 'forbidding' is a nastier verb.

We are influenced by threat of loss

Framing something as a loss or a gain can influence people's decision-taking. Generally speaking, we experience stronger feelings about the threat of loss than the prospect of gain. Our reactions are more intense. Someone already occupying the role of a world sports champion has an inherent advantage over any challenger to the role, precisely because of this reason. If the current world champion loses, generally speaking, the public will feel the loss more strongly than the gain. The feeling of supporters, of course, will be determined by where their loyalties lie.

When we think we are going to gain something we are less likely to take risks than if we think we are going to lose something. So if your remit is to persuade the board of a company to take a radical course of action, then persuading them that they will lose, say, market share to their greatest rival if they do not follow this action will be a more effective argument than trying to persuade them that if they follow this course of action, they will gain market share.

This guideline applies in all sorts of contexts. In health education, when women are warned what they will lose if they don't carry out breast self-examinations, they are more likely to undertake them than if they are told what they will gain. It's the appeal of fear – a great motivator.

And, consequently, eliminating risk is a powerful carrot in decision-taking. If people are told it takes £10 to reduce a risk by half, and then £20 to eliminate the risk, the great majority will opt for the second option. In the same way – and we are rather extreme about all this, aren't we? – we would rather have something for free than have a percentage taken off something. So a greengrocer who sells four peaches, with one of the four free, will have a lot more success with her special offer than the one that offers 25 percent off four peaches.

In the music business it's often said that the only way to get concrete commitment to a deal is through scaring the record company into believing that a rival company is going to get the act. I suspect there may be some truth in this for getting people to commit to all sorts of things – such as making television programmes, publishing books and giving promotions. And you're almost certain to be familiar with the ploy estate agents use with a 'Well, we've actually got somebody else interested in the property' in order to get action on commitment.

Instantly irresistible

- When you're after a job, it's worth thinking through beforehand what qualities the employers will be missing out on, if they fail to hire you. Obviously, the closer these are to what they see as essentials of the role, the better. Highlight as much as possible instances of you using these qualities.

- When you're making a case for a course of action, it's important to highlight the pluses as well as the minuses. By all means serve up the minuses early on and in clear terms, but people need to hear the positives, too. If you influence people consistently through emphasising what they might lose, then you are influencing through fear. This may paralyse these people and make them less effective. At some level, too, these people will be moving away from you, because you're scaring them – and they certainly ain't going to want to get any closer.

We are influenced by optimism

When you are a risky choice, or putting a risky case, you will be better served by a decision-taker in an optimistic mood. When I studied decision-making at university, a most entertaining lecturer used to sum up the subject by saying, 'It's pessimists that make the best decisions.' What he meant was that we are often more rational in a pessimistic rather than an optimistic mood. Here's an example:

You and your partner are discussing where to go on holiday. You have both had terrific days at work – lots of excitement and good deals. The weather is glorious so you adjourn to a very pleasant wine bar. You start to discuss the Maldives as an option, and start to enjoy visualising yourselves swimming in cobalt blue waters, sipping Sea Breezes, wallowing in the secluded luxury. This is your expensive option. Then you move to discuss your cheap option: the Lake District. A couple of thoughts on the joys of Lake Windermere and the two of you return to discuss your Maldive paradise. Ah, what the hell, you're both doing well at work, you're both feeling terrific – why not plump for paradise? Your optimistic, feel-good moods have made the decision for you.

When we decision-take we will often discuss best and worst case scenarios, and if we feel particularly optimistic then we will want to spend more time on the former. We will take more risks on this best case scenario, because it is attractive and makes us feel good. This feel-good factor is tremendously important in politics and in business. To my mind both Tony Blair and Bill Clinton got elected because they symbolised hope: something we all need and which makes us feel good.

At the time of writing, I'm involved in a research project at London University, where the researchers are analysing techniques used by charismatic business speakers, like Tom Peters and Rosabeth Moss Kanter. What they convey above all else is a passion and commitment, which people in their audiences get carried along with. Audience members accept these speakers as leaders and authorities, identify strongly with them and then start to feel the same emotions of passion and commitment that the speakers are expressing.

In business, 'business confidence' is often mentioned. What this means is that people in general feel optimistic, so are taking riskier decisions and buying more impulsively and more. When business confidence falls, it means that there is generally a pessimistic mood, and so people are thinking through their buying decisions beforehand. In a pessimistic mood, we are more likely to consider cons then pros, and to succumb to primacy effect in our decisions. So, no sale.

Instantly irresistible

- Asking for something considerable? Then try to time your decisions so that the decision-maker is feeling optimistic – just after great trading figures have been announced, or after she's come back from a rejuvenating holiday.

- People who feel hugely enthusiastic and passionate and committed about their homing pigeons, or their toyboy lover or their vegan cooking abilities, can find it very difficult to project the same degree of verve when trying to convince the board to overhaul IT systems, or talking about their job experience in a job interview. It can help to talk about your enthusiasm first into a tape recorder, and then with the same momentum, move into talking about the work-related stuff. Play it back and if there's a big difference, analyse what you're doing in the first excerpt that you could do more of in the second.

Group decisions

In certain situations where your irresistibility is important, you will be trying to influence groups.

And, as individuals, we behave slightly differently in groups than we do alone.

Some of us are guilty of what's been called 'social loafing'. Now this doesn't mean lurking around the photocopier episodically in the vain hope that Hubert from Operations will come by to do his thing. No, what this involves is feeling that we don't need to put in quite so much effort in group activities because there isn't as direct a connection between effort and result as there is when we do things alone.

Practically, then, this translates into the idea that if you've met a person individually, and they've arranged for you to visit to influence a group of which they are a member, don't rely on them to react as enthusiastically as they did in the one-on-one situation. The individual could be a social loafer.

Psychological research takes this idea further, examining the extent to which we help one another as members of a group. There are all sorts of horrible instances of people collapsing on tube platforms or being viciously and audibly attacked on the street, while no one goes to help. This is another worrying instance of social loafing: as a member of a large group of passers-by, we take less responsibility for events than if we were the only person around.

Another phenomenon that's been the object of psychological research is called 'groupthink' – when groups take bad decisions because of certain features of the group. The example that's always cited is the Bay of Pigs fiasco, where the USA government group headed up by John Kennedy decided to invade Cuba. This decision, which turned out to be a bad one, was made without sufficient research and analysis of what was really going on.

Groupthink occurs when the group is united and self-contained, when it is very confident and certain of its rightness and when 'mindguards' protect the group from information that might challenge its smugness. You can easily see, I think, how a group of self-consciously powerful individuals might form themselves into such a group. Where you're trying to influence such a group, or if you suspect that you are involved in groupthink at work, you can counteract the effect by encouraging criticism, bringing in people from the outside and inviting other parties to come up with solutions to the problems under discussion.

Research with juries shows that groups tend to polarise in their decision-making. So if a jury is presented with weak evidence for a case, they will pass a more lenient judgement than each of the individuals involved would have done if they had been asked to judge on their own. Or if they are presented with a strong case, then their collective judgement tends to be harsher than it would have been individually. Groups are also cruder than individuals in pigeon-holing people; if someone suggests on superficial evidence that they fit into an

'IT nerd' category or a 'corporate amazon' one, then they will quickly be accepted as such – more quickly and readily than if they were interacting with group members one-to-one.

Just one final point about group decision-making. If you're in charge of the group and powerful, you will get better collective decision-making if you refrain from stating your personal position at the outset. People will be less likely to go along with what you say because you are *numero uno*. And if you want your group members to brainstorm ideas – to come up with random solutions however wacky – this is best done with them brainstorming individually and then bringing their ideas to the group discussion. Done *in situ*, in the group, this system just favours the uninhibited.

Persuading groups irresistibly

Where your aim is to persuade a group of people, which usually means that you have a specified time span within which to achieve your goal, it's wise to be as tactical in your thinking as you can beforehand.

Research your audience

It's sensible to research your target audience as much as possible and to consider all their prejudices, biases and expectations. Rather than ignoring these, you may find people listen in a much more receptive mode when these influences are openly acknowledged. Try something along the lines of: 'Now I know the past three occasions I've asked for money for this project you've turned me down, but I'm hoping today to persuade you that circumstances are such, now, that the project's irresistible to you . . .'

This illustrates another tactic: rather than trying to covertly persuade people, it's useful to . . .

Be upfront about your aim

Be very clear in your mind, even if you don't make it explicit, what's in it for your specific audience, in terms of both benefits and threats. Hook them in early with the most important of these. Triggers that may persuade people include:

- psychological benefits – for instance, many of us give to charity because we feel better about ourselves
- threats – we've already discussed some of these, including fear and loss
- money – people may be persuaded to do things for financial gain, because of aspiration to be as good as or better than a peer group
- sex, greed, physical comfort and just because something is new and novel

While you may be making the benefits of your case very explicit, you may want to be more cautious about the downside, but with answers ready to handle objections. When people are objecting heavily, keep pushing the benefits relentlessly. And sum these up once more at the end, to take advantage of recency effect (see page 179).

Helpful heuristics

Some other influences on how persuasive we are come from what psychologists call heuristics: factors that affect our decision-making. One of these is *availability*. This means that if we have heard of something happening – say, in the newspapers or through gossip – then we are more likely to believe it will happen again. So if someone is persuading you to join their lottery syndicate and you have, in the past month, read about five different lottery winners in the newspaper, then you are more likely to join that syndicate than if you hadn't read the stories. Ah, now you know why the tabloids periodically do stories about lottery winners. And now you know why you should subtly allude to any recent successes you may have had in your life, or any good publicity you have received.

Another heuristic is *vividness*. This means that when we hear information that is more detailed and vivid, we are more likely to believe it to be true. Some researchers in America – Reyes, Thompon and Bower – illustrated this in 1980 with the best-titled psychological experiment ever:

THE CASE OF THE GUACAMOLE.

They gave jury members two illustrations of a case description. The first was pallid: 'On his way out of the door, Sands (the defendant) staggered against a serving table, knocking a bowl to the floor.' The second was gloriously green and vivid: 'On his way out of the door, Sands staggered against a serving table, knocking a bowl of guacamole dip to the floor and splattering guacamole on the white shag carpet.' Immediately after hearing this, there was no difference in the jury's perception of Sands' guilt. But forty-eight hours later, they were much more likely to believe that he was guilty from the second description than the first. The vividness and specific detail had entered their memories and affected their judgement. They could see vivid spicy guacamole spattered all over the white shag carpet – in the manner of the shower curtain in *Psycho*, I suspect. And we all remember the vivid nature of that scene!

Vivid scenarios and description, along with some interesting detail, make for irresistible persuasion. So it's worth thinking about where the metaphorical guacamole is in your career history, and what vividness you can bring to positive outcomes for cases for which you are fighting.

The final heuristic I want to mention is called *anchoring*. This means that when we want to persuade others of anything, we will be influenced by estimates and positions that we have previously received. Researchers conducted an experiment with experienced estate agents who were given houses to value. For some of the properties they were also given details of previous estimates of the value of each property. These previous estimates were either particularly inflated or lower than expected. In every instance, the estate agents valued the properties closer to the 'anchoring' estimate, where they had been given one. For the properties where there had been no previous anchor, the prices were close to the real market value.

We use this guideline with one another all the time in negotiation. We stake out an extreme position and then expect to be cajoled from there into something that is more favourable to both parties. When we are persuading others it's worth looking for opportunities to mention something that's considerably more than you're actually after – to anchor the listener's consciousness in the right direction. Remember that if you are discussing the best that can happen and the worst that can happen, you want to run the discussion in that order so that the anchor works for the positive. For example, if you want to get some investment for a project, the right way to do this is to talk about the profits and benefits first, and then to mention the loss of kudos if you don't go ahead, rather than reversing the order.

Making brilliant decisions

I couldn't finish this chapter without mentioning a few pointers about making brilliant decisions on your own behalf. As I'm sure you know, you maximise your irresistibility when you choose to do things that suit you best. Here we go:

Use logic and intuition

Of course it's sensible to gather facts and evidence and to weigh up the pros and cons before you make a decision. When you're making a decision such as choosing between two flats to buy, it's almost certainly worth creating two columns, one for flat A and one for flat B. List on one side of the page criteria you are looking for in a flat, giving those criteria numbers in terms of importance from 1 to 5. Then rank each flat in terms of how it satisfies the criteria, and the criteria numbers by the satisfaction numbers, to give a comparison.

But also listen to your intuition, which is fast and subconscious logical analysis. When we react intuitively we experience leaps of connections between neurons, which create intuitive feelings. It's rather like meeting someone with whom you instantly feel at ease – your mind has made associations with individuals you've met in the past with the same qualities. But your intuitive reaction will happen much quicker than your conscious analysis of those qualities could. Literally, this might be a gut reaction. There are cells in the stomach that carry neuro-transmitters that react to emotion. Go with it – it's usually right.

Imagine the opposite

If you suspect you are being influenced by anchoring heuristics – someone trying to get you to pay a high price for something – then spend some time imagining the opposite, paying a low price for it. With a prospective property purchase, you could do this by going back to view it, with a much lower figure in mind. Wander around again and decide whether it's good value at this lower price.

Ask disconfirming questions

You are being shown round a prospective place of employment and you suspect everyone is working terribly hard – perhaps too hard – to convince you what a happy place it is to work. So, rather than seeking confirming evidence, with a question like 'So it's a happy place to work then?', seek disconfirming evidence with 'Is it true it's an unhappy place to work?' When people are selling you something hard, ask them the opposite of what they are trying to confirm, and watch their reactions closely . . .

Get gloomy

There are times in life when it's useful to get gloomy. If you are making an important decision, be aware of the influences of mood. In a state of high optimism you may take greater risks and only see positive future scenarios. Delay taking the decision until you are feeling less buoyant and can consider what could go wrong.

Take the short- and the long-term view

Giving up alcohol might be horrendous over the next week, but just think what it'll do for those veins on your nose over the long term.

I find this whole business of decision-taking fascinating. There are so many psychological influences on it. I hope this chapter's given you useful insights into how people decide about you, and also made you aware of some of the pitfalls to avoid when taking decisions yourself.

So that's it – decision time over. And while you decide whether to read on, I've decided to finish this chapter. Toodle-pip.

7

From No to Flow

I hate that word 'No'. It can be among the most painful words in our language – especially when it's followed by messages like, 'I don't want to continue this relationship', 'You didn't get the job' or 'We don't want to use your services'. When we want something very badly, then plan how to get it and fantasise how wonderful life will be when we do, the rejection can come as a terrible blow. So terrible for some of us, that it puts us off ever risking rejection and failure again. We insulate ourselves against the risk by avoiding close relationships, or never trying anything new, or living very dull lives. We may never try to be – or believe ourselves to be – irresistible again.

In my view, the art of living well is about balancing the ideas inside our own heads against the feedback and evidence we get from others. It's important to be receptive and sensitive to the re-actions of others, otherwise we have no barometer to gauge how close our interpretation of events is to reality. But when we're vague or unsure about our own ideas, we may become hyper-sensitive to external feedback. We may take criticism and rejection very personally. And, of course, becoming irresistible involves offering ourselves to others repeatedly, with inevitable rejection. So if this is our aim, then we have to have an attitude towards rejection that serves us well.

Among the worst sorts of rejection is that which comes from a parent to a child. When we are small we look to our parents to give us our identity and tell us who we are. If our parents have told us that we are worthless, bad and unattractive, and we (inevitably) believe this to an extent, then our fear of rejection is likely to be quite high.

I mentioned earlier in this book that my mother was mentally unstable for quite a lot of my upbringing. My grandmother was put in a lunatic asylum when my mother was eight, and for the subsequent six years my mother had no idea where she'd gone. My mother was obsessed with abandonment and rejection. She and I didn't have a very good relationship, despite my efforts to make it so.

While my father tried very hard – and succeeded to an extent – to counter her demolition of my confidence, a legacy remains. I know I'm more sensitive than I need to be about rejection. Though I rationalise it in my work, I hate inviting people to social events, particularly over the phone, in case they say no. I get nervous about it and I put it off. I'm always very relieved when I've made the invitation and they've accepted. This is ridiculous really, as our family are sociable people and usually everybody we invite to our parties wants to come. Whenever my parents entertained, which fortunately wasn't very often, my mother would get into the most terrible paddy. I remember this well.

But enough introspection from you, author, I hear you cry. What about us, your readers? And what will you do for us in this chapter? Well, in this chapter we look at how to create a constructive attitude towards rejection. We look at how to handle fear of failure and at how we motivate ourselves through using criticism well. We'll also examine goal-setting and the secret of fulfilment – something called 'Flow'. All the ideas in the chapter are vital to you becoming your own best self-development coach, and they will all help you to become irresistible.

This chapter will be particularly useful if you put things off, or talk about your ideas a lot but never actually do anything about them because deep down inside you're scared of failing. It will be useful, too, if you tend to adopt a cynical attitude about a lot of things. We become cynical when hope dies. So we develop cynical attitudes when we have been very hopeful about something that never came to fruition. To protect and defend us from that ever happening again we will pour scorn on our own potential, and the dreams and potential of other people.

A cynical attitude is a complete dead end that

takes a person nowhere. It stops them growing, learning and connecting with the ever-changing environment. In that respect, it's not very clever. And it's certainly not irresistible.

Handling rejection

An act of rejection can be like an expandable piece of baggage. It hurts you at the time so you start to carry the memory around like a small duffle bag. Then, as more of life's experiences get interpreted as further evidence to add to this memory, so you expand it into a spacious shoulder bag. Then before you know it, the memory's become a whopping great rucksack. Five years on, after the event, the memory has become an enormous unwieldy trunk, full of evidence that the bad things you decided about human nature at the time are right. Sisters and brothers, you need to lighten that load.

Keep the rejection specific

When we find rejection traumatic, we may generalise wildly from the experience. So if a boyfriend dumps us, then 'all men are unreliable'; if an interviewer is horrid 'all interviewers are sadists'; if someone from a particular industry doesn't give us business, then that sector's not for us. All these experiences are one-offs, and unlikely to be predictors of responses from the entire category.

It's often helpful to regard the rejection as being about specifics, too, as one aspect of our behaviour that is being spurned, rather than our entire being. We were rejected from the job interview because we didn't have the right experience in the past. Hubert in Operations didn't want to prolong the relationship because we were too interested in the arts. We didn't get the promotion we were after because we weren't a specialist in the particular area they were looking for.

Now this doesn't mean flying in the face of any feedback you've been given. If a debrief following an unsuccessful job interview tells you that you were under-skilled for a role, then clearly you can do something about this. But sometimes people may be unable or reluctant to express why they are rejecting you – in which case, find a specific rather than interpreting it as a global condemnation of who you are. Sometimes you may need to do this via guesswork, checking out your ideas with others. Sometimes it may be appropriate to press for as much specific feedback as you can get, asking people what they think you should do more or less of.

It's my view that most rejection does tend to be about specifics anyway, rather than about whole beings. As whole beings we are complex, deep and difficult to know. I doubt whether any of us are ever well-equipped with enough knowledge of another person to reject them on the basis of the whole person. But then, as a psychologist, I would believe that, wouldn't I? Otherwise, what would I have to study?

Maybe it just wasn't meant to be

This means thinking along the lines of: if you had taken that job, shacked up with Hubert or taken that promotion, it might have meant missing something exciting around the corner. This relates to an idea to which I don't really subscribe, which is that our fate is predestined. Now our future is shaped to some extent through the influence of our genes, and expectations we get from our conditioning. But luck and chance events play a role, too. In my view, there is no grand plan for each and every one of us. When we believe there is, it can often lull us into spending our lives in the passenger's seat, rather than that of the driver.

The 'maybe it just wasn't meant to be' idea is a sustaining philosophy based on the idea that in most circumstances, there are other opportunities to seek out. If these opportunities seem thin on the ground, then you may need to broaden the territories in which you seek them. This idea often keeps the most successful salespeople and tenacious entrepreneurs going. If they miss a sale or an opportunity, they see no point wallowing in present failure, but resolve to move on and be inventive about finding future opportunities. You can apply this guideline to finding partners, jobs or business. Here's Richard's story:

> I work in a fairly upmarket estate agents – well, someone has to – and once a week our manager organises a tour of new properties we've acquired, so we know what we're selling. I was finding business hard, the property market was sluggish and despite all my efforts on behalf of clients, I didn't seem to be shifting much. Anyway, I turned up with two of my colleagues outside a new property we'd acquired, for the weekly viewing. A middle-aged couple were standing outside, admiring it. Rather than dash in with the other two, I engaged them in conversation. They said that they'd often admired the house and would be interested in viewing. I asked the vendor if they minded me showing them around. At the end of the viewing, I suggested that if they were interested in buying the house they should pop into the office later that day. My colleagues teased me all the way back to the office, because of my optimism. But on arrival back at base, they were taken aback, as the middle-aged couple were waiting to do business. That was our agency's first 24-hour sale and I've trusted my instincts ever since. This approach allows me to be creative and inventive in a profession that is hardly renowned for these qualities – only in connection with handling the truth.

Is another route indicated?

Sometimes, it's worth asking yourself what goal the rejection prevents you from reaching. So, a failed job interview may mark a blip on your path to professional success; a rejection in a relationship is an obstacle towards getting a long-lasting partnership and family life; a failed business pitch is a setback in your dream of running your own successful enterprise. Clarify your goal, and work out all the different ways of reaching it.

And there will be alternative routes you could take towards your goals: writing personally to someone who could give you a great job and asking to meet them, using a dating agency to meet more potential partners, creating a new shop window for your business, which will encourage prospective clients to come to you.

Reframing the memory

This idea involves you playing the role of a film director. You are taking unhelpful memories and refilming them so that their detrimental effect on you is minimised. You can be as creative and imaginative as you like in the scenarios and detail you conjure up. More often than not, you'll be refilming a tragedy and turning it into a comedy. Here's an example of this:

> John was a university lecturer who, inevitably, was experienced and confident speaking to groups of people. There was some industrial unrest at his university and he was asked to go along and talk to a large gathering of union members and

officials. He barely gave it a thought, thinking that
the audience would respond to him in the way his
students did. They would accord him expert
power, and listen to his voice of authority.

But, as you've probably guessed, they didn't.
They interrupted, argued and disrupted his case.
The whole experience was horribly humiliating for
him. And every time, subsequently, that he had to
address an outside meeting, this incident would
loom large in his mind, in vivid technicolour.

Were John to refilm this incident, he could do the
following. He could replay the incident mentally,
seeing his attackers as very small, and himself as
very large. He could see himself getting hurt, but
then walking away, uninjured, healthy and hearty,
ready to fight another day.

Or if he wanted to take another, more imaginative approach, he might replay the incident as
slapstick. He could throw custard pies at his
union attackers, see them getting absolutely splat-
tered, watch them slip everywhere on the custardy
floor, while he sits there, calm and composed. Then
when they're all flat on the floor, he could just walk
away into the sunlight into a different welcoming
situation.

All of these ideas are mental games to help us
change the character of a memory, because we
never know whether memories are accurate or not.
I have used this method with great success on a
matter that hurt me a lot. An associate of mine
defected, and tried to poach a lot of my clients, after

I'd considered I'd done a great deal to help her. I felt very injured and unjustly treated. I created a mental film of her departure from my company. It was a very beautiful rural setting, with abundant and lush flora on the banks surrounding a calm glimmering river. The miscreant was floating down the river, into the distance, like the Lady of Shallot in the J.W. Waterhouse painting. Eventually she disappeared altogether, while I sat relaxed and serene on the river bank, with a sort of benign magnificence about me, as I watched her go. And yes, because you could be wondering, she was stiff as a board, since rigor mortis had set in.

Create a constructive goal out of rejection

When an act of rejection has upset and left you feeling sensitive, you can create a constructive goal out of the experience. Let's take some examples: the disastrous job interview that leaves you feeling that you're never going to go to a job interview again, because interviewers are savage, can be converted into a goal for you to become really good at interviewing techniques. The response that says you're never going to enter into a relationship again, because women are completely emotionally unpredictable, can become a goal to find a woman who is as rational as you are. Yes, I assure you they do exist.

And the humiliation at a board meeting that

leaves you vowing you will never present to the board again can be converted into a goal to learn to be dispassionate about and effective at presenting.

Desensitise yourself

Realistically, there are some places in life where there is a huge amount of rejection – any roles where glamour, fame and large amounts of money feature, for instance. So, if you've decided to manage or become the next Madonna, or write a best-seller, or become the top bond dealer in the City of London, then you are playing in the most competitive fields, where there is much more rejection than acceptance. Your goal will need to be important enough that it will enable you to handle this.

Rather like a fear-of-flying course, where you become desensitised to the situation, it can be very helpful to leap in and deliberately put yourself in situations where you are likely to be rejected. Rosalind described this experience:

By chance, I did this when I first came to London after university. I got a really humiliating job, going round people's offices trying to sell them shirts from a large and heavy bag full of the things. At the end of week two, I was seventeen pounds down, as I'd lost one shirt and sold none. I gave that up, got a waitressing job and tried to pursue my real passion, which was acting.

Now acting is a terrible business to go into if you fear rejection. But the six years I tried it anaesthetised me towards rejection and taught me to be philosophical about it. Not able to get a good acting agent, I joined a co-operative agency, run by the actors themselves. I got insight into how to run a small business and how people cast things – in other words, how the market worked. There was great camaraderie over collectively felt rejection. When one person got turned down for a role, the rejection was depersonalised and we all took it on board.

When I decided to leave the acting profession, I felt very philosophical about rejection. Starting my catering business I used to think, 'Oh what the hell, if they don't want my services, I'll move on to somebody else who does, and just keep widening the net to try and find customers.' It worked. Some people would view the years I spent acting as a waste of time, but I didn't. It prepared me so well to be philosophical about rejection when it came to building my business.

There's a big 'so what' element about all this. And when you're facing a lot of rejection that phrase should be uppermost in your mind. If somebody turns you down for a job, *so what* – there are others out there. When someone turns down your living-together proposal, *so what* – there are other partners out there. If someone says they don't want to buy your services, then *so what* – someone else will benefit from whatever it is you're selling.

Remember the upside of surviving the 'no'

The more you learn to survive the 'no', the greater your courage and the more you will achieve. And the greater your achievement, the more choices you will be able to make – about what you do, who you do it with, where you live, what you eat and even where you go on holiday. So in learning to survive the 'no', we get chances to say 'no' to choices that are offered us a bit more often.

I'm not suggesting you be motivated by revenge here – though the Welsh have a vendetta tradition that thrives every bit as well as the Italians'. The point is that you get more choices, and you may be saying 'yes' as often as 'no'.

Making a friend of failure

It's so horrible failing: dodgy exam results, failing to get a job you really want, divorce, your child failing to get into a great school, or coming last in an election. I could go on but I won't; I'm not aiming to depress you, dear reader. And although that's the way many of us react to failure – with a slightly depressed feeling in our stomachs – there are some people for whom it almost becomes a best friend.

People can become very attached to fear of failure because it keeps them looking good. They never lose face, never risk shame or humiliation, or the harsh judgement of others. On planet 'Fear of Failure', everything is dull, predictable and safe. No one ever tries anything so nothing ever goes wrong. Life is stultifying and quietly desperate. Other people may keep their distance, because there is something slightly inhuman about people who never fail.

Sometimes, in order to keep fragile self-worth intact, a person will deliberately ensure they fail, by creating the right external circumstances. Take Sally, for example:

> Sally's about to sit an exam, and she is terrified of trying her best and failing. So to ensure this doesn't happen, she does absolutely no revision. She knows this will maximise the possibility of failure. But it's failure that can be blamed on her lack of preparation, rather than her intrinsic ability. So she maintains that fragile self-worth.

Fear of failure can be caused by other people looking after us, and taking on the role of our protectors. When a little girl or boy, let's call them Joanna and Timmy, is shy or timid, a parent may have a vested interest in keeping them so. You'll often hear a parent say things like, 'Oh, don't ask Joanna to sing, she's very shy,' or 'Don't expect Timmy to go on the slide, he's petrified,' endorsing what the parent wants to be true. In keeping little Joanna or Timmy shy or timid, it means that the child will stay dependent on the parent for much longer than if he or she had been encouraged to become independent. It's in the parent's interests to keep them this way. Sometimes these children never become independent and end up living at home well into adulthood, unable to form close relationships with other adults.

When we decide to tackle our fears, then the balance of power in our relationships may shift. It often happens with married couples when the wife decides to return to work, after a few years at home with the children. She'll decide to reinvent herself, and to become more confident. The husband may find all this rather disquieting and feel resentful, having secretly rather enjoyed having the little woman at home to cater for his every whim. He'd secretly like her to worry about failure, to the extent that she'll remain reliant on him. Like Joanna and Timmy's parents, he's motivated to nurture this fear.

So these are the pay-offs for keeping our friend failure alive and well. We always look good and keep others happy. Now, as you might expect, I'm going to offer you a great big juicy carrot for tackling this fear of failure – something that far outweighs the advantages of staying scared.

The fighting fear carrot

You only have one life. At least, that's what I believe. So you owe it to yourself to make the most of it, and to act with enlightened self-interest (that is, due consideration of others). If you don't confront your fear and do something about it, then that lurking unease about whatever it is you're scared of will stay with you all your life.

Now some fear of failure is a good thing. But you don't want to have buckets of it, which prevents you from doing anything. If we didn't know what failure was, we wouldn't recognise achievement. You can't have one without the other. We would never experience the exhilaration of accepting and tackling a challenge. We would never experience the wonderful sense of achievement of having wrestled with our little fear demons and overcome them.

So there's a good trade-off going on here. In exchange for worrying about failure, but still risking it, we are able to grow – to learn new things about ourselves and our environment, to under-stand others better and to gain wisdom. And it is the sense of purpose and courage with which we tackle our fear of failure that makes us irresistible to others.

Motivating yourself after rejection

So here am I banging on about how to increase your irresistibility, and you're probably thinking, 'Yes, but I just can't be bothered,' or 'Some days I don't feel like getting out of bed, let alone embarking on a self-improvement programme.' Knowing how to motivate yourself, especially if you're in the early aftermath of surviving rejection, is essential.

Now one of the key things to get right in life in order to be a happy – and successful – bunny is the match between our own perceptions of what is going on and what is really happening in *objective reality*. This blissful state, objective reality, may be extremely difficult to get a handle on – and the closest approximation we will often be able to get of it is through other people's opinions. So this means receiving, accepting and using criticism constructively.

And when we get on to the touchy subject of criticism, it's most useful to start with self-criticism. For many of us it's an expert art, because we have had so much practice at it.

Constructive self-criticism

With little knowledge about such matters around, many of today's adults were brought up to receive very little praise. For instance, it wasn't until a couple of years after my mother died that I realised that part of the reason why I was being very self-critical was in order to try to please her. All this when she was no longer on the planet, and I knew that whatever I achieved her pleasure would have been at best grudging.

Being highly self-critical can be very demotivating, because that noisy little voice inside our head will often sabotage our performance. The inner critic will be conditioned to give us negative messages rather than positive ones during events like presentations, interviews and meetings. We may hear our inner critic saying things like 'You're being inarticulate', 'You're boring people', 'People are thinking you're fat' or 'Everyone's noticing you're over forty'.

This critical voice *can* become a great friend to us, and help us act as our own best coaches. It can set goals for us and help us improve our performance to achieve those goals. But it has to learn to give positive messages first, and then to give negative ones. Without these positive messages we give ourselves nothing constructive on which to build. And as any coach worth his team's strip will tell you, people have to know what they're doing well, before they can improve their weaknesses.

Instantly irresistible

- When you want to do well in a situation, review your performance as soon as you can. Note down in two columns: a) what went well and b) where there was scope for improvement.
- Restrict your inner critic to analysing your performance in terms of verbs; that is, what you *did*, rather than condemning yourself for life through adjectives and nouns (of the 'you were a boring prat' variety). So you might end up with: you spoke

fluently and you convinced people in column a) and, in column b), you cited too many statistics and sounded a bit nervous at the beginning. When your inner critic uses verbs to criticise, you can choose to *do* something different next time.

- Give your inner critic days off. Or, if you can't do that, then the odd hour. Even inner critics need rest days, in order to recharge their critical faculties. It's very easy if you work long hours – and when your performance matters a great deal to you – to keep that inner critic constantly active. Take a break.

- In very important situations you want to turn that inner critic off completely. This is to allow all of your attention to go into what the situation requires you to *do* rather than being obsessed about how you're coming across, and what people think of you. We're back to that key idea of being clear about intention. Afterwards, you can switch your critic back on to review what happened.

- When you're going through a rough patch in life, treat yourself for a day or two – or even longer if you dare – and get the inner critic stuck on positives. Treat yourself so that you only allow that inner voice to praise you.

Other people's criticism

In my work, I notice that the higher people get in their organisations the more difficult it is for them to get genuine, useful criticism, untainted by jealousy or political tactics. On the plus side, I suppose, this gives plenty of work to consultants who are ready to do that very thing.

This may be glaringly obvious, but you will get useful criticism if you ask for it. Most of us don't do this because we are hyper-sensitive to the stuff. As soon as someone says something that could imply criticism, and especially if the comments are true, then we will stop listening and justify their criticism by blaming other people and factors outside our control. Nothing to do with me, governor.

The risk of loss of face from admitting we've got things to learn, or that we could have done better in some way, is just too great. But the risk of ignoring criticism is greater. We can end up operating in a vacuum, having lost touch with reality, disconnected from what others really think of our ideas and performance.

Though I know it may sound like an act of self-flagellation, it makes great sense to ask people, whose opinion you trust, for criticism. And make it the constructive kind. They, too, can act as a coach.

Instantly irresistible

- You could ask someone for criticism on a quid pro quo basis; you know, 'You scratch my back, and I'll scratch yours.' Suggest to them that if they'd like feedback (the nice word for criticism) on anything, you'd be happy to give it.

- So, before an event, be very specific to your critic about what you are trying to do and use verbs again. So rather than 'I'm trying to be more authoritative to the chief exec', describe specific behaviour they can look out for, like 'I'm going to try to use short sentences and state clearly the pros and cons'. Then they will know exactly what to monitor.
- Try to get their comments as soon as possible after the event. And thank them for their interest!
- When the people around you would be embarrassed by a direct request for feedback – and this means a lot of places in England – then phrase your request as an exercise for their imaginations. So, you might want to say something along the lines of, 'If you were running that meeting and putting that case would you have done it any differently?' You'll usually find that people will express themselves very freely. What they are effectively giving you is criticism, but it doesn't feel as direct as that, to either party.

Unexpected criticism

Is there any way you can deal constructively with that dollop of criticism that's lobbed at you completely out of the blue? Well, yes. Instead of shouting, 'That's ridiculous,' and stomping out of the room, here are some ideas to make that unexpected lob a useful one.

Listen to what the person is saying, even if you think their comments are farcical, because it gives some insight into their psychology in terms of their priorities. We only criticise people on the basis of what's important to us. And make sure you are clear about what the person is saying. If they are embarrassed they may be less articulate than usual. If you work closely together, the exchange may help you to cultivate a better relationship. Again, the guideline is find out specifically what it is you were *doing* that caused the comments.

If you have the slightest suspicion that the criticism might be useful, acknowledge that you've heard it. This doesn't mean accepting it – just letting the person know it's been received with an 'Oh, right, well I'll go away and think about that' or 'That's useful to know; I'll mull over it'.

When you suspect someone's motives, or they give that most pernicious form of criticism with a 'We've all been talking and what we think is . . .' then check it out with others for accuracy. People sometimes self-appoint themselves group spokespeople out of malice, when no group discussion has occurred.

And, remember, you can choose whether to accept or reject criticism and whether to act on it. What someone will see as a vice, others may regard as a virtue. I'm impatient for example – but I would prefer to regard this as decisive.

Erroneous beliefs

Sometimes rejection hits us extra hard because we live our lives according to erroneous beliefs about the world. When these beliefs are contradicted by what we experience, we will feel disappointed, frustrated and confused. I don't need to tell you that these feelings are very demotivating. These beliefs can only be about three things: ourselves, other people and the world we live in. I like to call these beliefs 'rogue rules', because while they can act as drivers to motivate us, when we apply them obsessively they will paralyse us into inaction.

These beliefs, applied rigidly, inevitably result in a fear of failure.

Being perfect

Beliefs or rules about perfection are very common. Along the lines of 'I must do everything perfectly, as should other people' and 'The world should be a perfect place'. When you're obsessively perfectionist, you will set yourself unrealistically high standards in many areas of your life and often feel disappointed when you fail to achieve them. You will criticise others for sloppiness and lack of attention to detail:

Janet came on a workshop because she felt that she was inarticulate in interviews and meetings. Yet, when she talked about what she did, she seemed to have an exceptionally fluent way of talking. Her appearance was very neat and well-groomed, and she said that she viewed herself as a perfectionist. She got upset with herself when she was nervous, because she felt that she couldn't always find exactly the right word for what she wanted to express. When we discussed what people on the receiving end of her communication were looking for, she acknowledged that she couldn't find a situation where they were being highly critical of her use of language. She needed to refocus her attention on whether people had got her meaning, and let that be a sufficient gauge of her effectiveness.

The world will never be a perfect place. Why, there is even a great body of chaos theory to read supporting the physics of it, if you're still convinced otherwise. With perfectionist tendencies, it's better to specialise in a couple of areas where you can impose order and work towards perfection, rather than trying to make yourself, and everybody else, live that way.

Perfectionism can demotivate us because we give ourselves messages like: 'No use trying; I won't be able to do it perfectly,' 'It's going to be chaotic while I'm learning and I won't be able to cope with that' or 'No thanks, I'll stay in my nice ordered little world.'

We can counter its bad effects through looking at the results of our actions, rather than the actions themselves. When you're not happy with something you've done or said, think about whether it's achieved the desired results. If it has, then you know you've been good enough.

Being fixed

This rogue rule can cause us to feel trapped and hopeless. It's based on a belief that there is far more fixity in the world than there actually is. Yes, of course, if you're born and raised in a sink estate, to a single mother with depression, living on benefit, then you are likely to have lower expectations than if you're born into a middle-class professional family. Rather alarming recent research from the Joseph Rowntree Foundation showed that these expectations could be shaped by the age of two. But circumstances and people *change*. Your body and brain is changing all the time, as is the world. And we should allow ourselves the flexibility to think ourselves into all kinds of situations.

When we get demoralised by a belief about fixity, we will get tunnel vision and limit our possibilities. We will be unable to see any route out of our predicament. In my experience, a bit of art can be helpful here. Drawing yourself in the context of everything that's happening around you in your world, and drawing the direction in which you want to take your life can be liberating. When we doodle we tend to be less self-censoring than when we write things down. Your doodles may generate ideas that you can then start taking practical steps to achieve.

The mobile society in which we live produces lots of examples of people who have achieved great things, despite their backgrounds. Bill Clinton came from a largely fatherless, poor Southern background. Oprah Winfrey was raised in poverty and deprivation. Bruce Oldfield, the British fashion designer, was a Barnardo's boy. Madeline Allbright, USA foreign affairs supremo, was born into a refugee Czechoslovakian family.

Being responsible, being liked, being a martyr

You will certainly be familiar with these common beliefs which can act as rogue rules: *I must take responsibility for everything. Other people should be more responsible. The world should reward me for being so responsible (with this rogue rule, you may find it impossible to delegate and to trust others. You may get over-stressed and exhausted through taking on too much).*

Or, *I must be liked by everyone. Everyone else wants to be liked as much as I do. The world must be a peaceful, harmonious place. (You will end up doing things you don't want to, because you've been afraid to disagree. But remember that you're not rejecting the person you disagree with – just their idea.)*

Or, *I must put everyone before myself. Other*

people should put my well-being before their own.
God – or somebody – will reward me for this some-
time in the future. (You'll end up being a chewed-up
doormat. Only lions love martyrs.)

These rules demotivate us because we place un-
realistic expectations on ourselves and others, and
because the world doesn't react in the way we
expect it to, because it doesn't know or plan how
it's going to behave.

Instantly irresistible

- When rogue rules are demotivating you, reason
  with them. Identify the rule, and then ask yourself
  whether you are trying to apply it in every situation and with all people. Identify situations where
  you can usefully make the rule important and ones
  where you can relegate it to little significance.
  Reinterpret these drivers as preferences that are
  useful but controlled motivators. For instance, 'I'd
  prefer reports that are written at work to be
  perfect, but I understand sometimes this might not
  be possible.' Or, 'I'd prefer the world to be harmonious, but I understand that sometimes – in order
  to achieve my goals – it may not be.'
- Deliberately flaunt your obsessive rules in un-
  important situations. You don't have to pack your
  supermarket trolley absolutely perfectly; you can
  change your mind about a social arrangement last
  minute; and you don't have to always express
  popular opinions in your reading group.

A final demotivator – not knowing yourself

It may well have struck you when you were reading the last section that these rogue rules are often at the heart of a person's self-image. We hear people say with pride that they're a perfectionist, responsible for three hundred people or a terrible victim of circumstance.

In self-help books, the message very often preached is: 'You can be anyone you want to be.' I'm of the view that this message needs tempering. If your view of yourself is very far removed from how everyone is interpreting you, then you may find yourself feeling confused and frustrated. You can be who you want to be – provided some outside feedback confirms this aim. Take Charlotte, for example:

Charlotte is a gentle, rather passive, kind and generous person who finds it difficult to express her emotions. She has a fantasy about herself as a tough cookie, a real mover and shaker, who strikes fear into the hearts of the indolent around her at work. She likes to recount tales of herself at work, featuring this fantasy behaviour. But I suspect none of us who know her well believe this to be credible. We indulge her because her virtues outweigh our scepticism.

Not comfortable with her real strengths, and not acknowledging them as such, Charlotte has difficulties forming close relationships. She is often misinterpreted by others, because they accept her fantasised version of herself and play tough back. She feels surprised and confused.

That's not to say fantasy is a bad thing. I'm all for it – in bucketfuls. It's often a great motivator, provided that others are accepting the version of yourself that you choose to project.

Going for goals

When we're not clear about our goals, we are much more likely to take rejection badly, and to feel a sense of failure. Clear goals give us a sense of direction, and also a philosophy that any knocks along the way are inevitable and survivable. The odd failure will seem relatively insignificant compared with the importance of the goals.

When we think about motivation there are two basics to consider: *what* motivates us and *how* we are motivated. There's been lots of research done into the *what* of motivation. Most widely quoted is Abraham Maslow, who said that people have a hierarchy of needs, through which they are motivated to ascend. Our lowest needs, he said, are for survival – things like food and shelter. Next up are our needs for love and relationships. And then, at the top of Maslow's hierarchy, is the need to self-actualise, rather vague in definition, but something to do with self-fulfilment.

A more down-to-earth analysis was done by Clayton Alderfer, who said that motivating needs could be categorised into needs for existence, which would include the basics for survival, needs for relatedness, love and all that stuff, and needs for growth, which could include psychological and spiritual development.

Without doubt, the most important idea to be clear about in terms of your individual motivation is what your priorities are. And these priorities are best clarified on the basis of your self-knowledge and the environment in which you live. Too many of us don't really think about our priorities in terms of what we want and what would make us happy; we go for things because the media is telling us that's the way we should live our lives, or because all of our friends are doing it. These priorities need reviewing regularly, to match the pace of change in ourselves and the environment.

The *how* of effective motivation is all about goals. The best sort of goal is one that's fairly challenging yet not too difficult – where there is a realistic chance of achieving the goal. If the goal is gargantuan, then we will be making unrealistically high expectations of ourselves, and risk becoming demotivated through disappointment.

When our goal is a pretty big one – losing two stone in my case – then we do best creating sub-goals on the way to achieving it (eight pounds every four weeks sounds about right, for me). And goals need to be set very specifically in terms of their timing, where they will occur, and what exactly they represent to us, in terms of how we feel.

We are more likely to achieve goals when we write them down and when we draw them. I like the latter approach especially, because pictures stay in our memories longer. It's most useful to visualise yourself achieving your goal, too, because the imagination is most potent in motivating us to keep trying.

Instantly irresistible

- Get clearer about your goals by asking yourself this question: if you had certain knowledge you were going to die in a year, what would you do or start to do now?
- What do you dream about in your life? Writing a novel, becoming a goddess, travelling the world? Get up half an hour earlier each morning and give that time to start to work on the goal. Plotting your epic, say, doing two hundred stomach squeezes, or researching cheap travel on the internet. You'll immediately start to feel more satisfied.

We need to keep checking that our goals are appropriate to the environment in which we're living and working. Here's Jim's story:

Jim worked in a finance department and knew he had potential to become head of the department and possibly head of the company. He drove himself relentlessly to become head of finance, and then devoted similar energy to becoming head of the company. But all this driving meant he had been keeping his head down, and had become blinkered. He'd failed to notice that marketing was now much more significant in the company, and when he threw his hat into the ring for the CEO's job, was appalled to find the board wanted a marketing expert in that role.

Goals get us up in the morning and give us a sense of purpose in life. They give us enthusiasm and energy and those are qualities that are irresistible. Goals also help us experience fulfilment, the subject of quite a lot of academic interest at the moment.

Flow – the secret of fulfilment

As we all know, it's much harder to concentrate when you are struggling with strong emotions or poor motivation. The great majority of us concentrate best when we are doing our favourite activity, be it gardening, striking a business deal or building a train set with a group of six-year-olds.

Professor Mihaly Csikszentmihalyi – try saying that after five gins – has studied the state where we find it easiest to concentrate and also where we feel most fulfilled. He calls this state 'flow'. In his book *Living Well: The Psychology of Everyday Life*, he describes this state as 'one that many people have used to describe the sense of effortless action they feel in moments that stand out as the best in their lives. Athletes refer to it as "being in the zone", religious mystics as being in "ecstasy", artists and musicians as aesthetic rapture. Athletes, mystics and artists do very different things when they reach flow, yet their descriptions of the experience are remarkably similar.'

The characteristics of this state are that it has a set of goals requiring certain reactions. The goals are clear and harmonious, so we get immediate feedback about how well we are doing. When someone's in a state of flow, the challenge is just about manageable and all the person's attention and skills are engaged in this challenge. Too high a challenge, and a person will get worried; too low a challenge and a person will get bored and demotivated.

In a state of flow, time passes very quickly and we do not experience anxiety or self-consciousness. We are not even aware of feeling happy. That sensation occurs afterwards, with our sense of achievement. And flow is an extremely motivating state, because we get it from mastering new skills and a sense of being completely engaged with what we are doing, to which we will want to return frequently.

Instantly irresistible

- To build your motivation and a sense of fulfilment, which others will find irresistible, organise your time to maximise periods of flow. You know, go with the flow to grow. And on that hippy-dippy note, let's go to the next chapter.

8

Relationship Selling

When we project irresistibility to others, we make them feel good about all sorts of things. We make them feel appreciated and considered and we bolster their sense of self-worth. At the heart of irresistibility lies the skill of affecting the way others feel.

In this chapter, I'd like to talk about three essential skills that help build irresistibility: managing our emotions, helping others to manage theirs and using emotional sense to get relationships going.

John is changing jobs at forty-five. He is nervous about his prospects because he thinks his age will count against him. But he dislikes it so much where he is that he feels he has no option. At his sixth interview, he meets a woman who had interviewed him twenty years previously. He hadn't got the job. He feels disheartened when he encounters her, taking it to be a bad omen. Two weeks later, he's thrilled to discover he's been given the job – partly because he had impressed her so much twenty years ago, even though she had felt in that instance that he was wrong for the role.

Sandra has decided to become self-employed. She is a marketing manager, and she wants to continue to give advice to drinks-industry clients, the type she's been familiar with over the past five years. She's slightly concerned about the security aspects of becoming self-employed but her fears are allayed by her biggest client assuring her that they will continue using her services. 'After all, we trust your judgement and you are so pleasant to deal with,' they comment.

A board of a company are choosing a new non-executive director. They have three well-qualified candidates in terms of experience and useful and interesting perspective. The one who is finally chosen is selected because she seems utterly trustworthy and to have a rapport with the company and its directors.

These are all examples of people using their feelings and memories of these feelings to give others great breaks. And, like every story in life, whether real or imaginary, they are to do with people making choices based on how they feel. And, of course, there is a massive contradiction here between how people really make decisions and attempting to free people of bias in circumstances like job selection panels. Bias always features in the way we react to others, and this bias is often to do with feelings.

Touchy-feely world

Since the 1960s, our culture has undergone a tremendous change in the nature of relationships. In 1950s Britain, very little was spoken or written about relationships. One either did or didn't do the right thing, and if the going got tough in a relationship, then one simply battened down the hatches, stiffened the old upper lip, and got on with things.

In millennium Britain, in contrast, the public expression of emotion has become heavily sanctioned. We've seen an alienated Princess Diana speaking on television about her feelings with regard to her own – and her husband's – adultery. Now how you judge the appropriateness of this may well be influenced by how comfortable you are expressing your emotions. My view is that we do need to be careful to avoid thinking that just because someone is able to articulate emotions, those emotions are justified and right – which is how I think a lot of people reacted to Princess Diana. Many others would have been affected by her very public expression of emotion – like her sons, for instance.

Years ago, when I studied drama, we student actors were all preoccupied with how we felt. Getting in touch with our emotions, and using them in characterisation, was the most important thing. We were incredibly interested in ourselves, every nuance of mood being important. We tended to have a great need for drama in our private lives and spent much of our time emoting to one another about these dramas. In short, we were self-obsessed luvvies – with a hugely inflated sense of our own significance.

In our lives, we experience what I believe to be defining moments: things that are done or said that cause big shifts in perspective. You may have some of these stored in your memory banks. One of my most memorable defining moments was to do with my feelings.

A few years after studying acting, I went to study to be a voice teacher and one of the subjects we studied was the Alexander Technique, which involves correcting posture, breathing and alignment. Our teacher was a marvellous woman called Glyn MacDonald. In truth, I found some of the classes boring, despite her considerable wisdom. At this stage, I was still in the 'if I feel it I must express it' phase, and so I would be deliberately disruptive if I felt bored. One day, she silenced me when I was objecting to something. She said, 'Stop asking yourself how you feel, and start asking yourself how you think.'

I knew that she had told me something profoundly relevant. I was so preoccupied with my own nuances of mood that I wasn't using my powers of logic and analysis nearly as much as I could. And because I was finding myself so interesting, I wasn't giving nearly enough attention to the big picture and the world around me. Glyn's advice was revelationary and timely, and I changed my life significantly as a result of it. When I looked out into the big picture, and thought about it, I realised there was a service I could provide that would be popular. So I started Voiceworks, my training company.

So while having 'emotional articulacy' is generally approved of in this day and age, it doesn't mean it should be indulged. Just being able to express how you are feeling doesn't mean that feeling is laudable. There are times when it's really useful to be able to control your emotions and to put your attention on to other people, and how they are feeling, instead.

Managing our emotions

Without doubt, one of the kindest things you can do to yourself to be a happy human being is to try to acknowledge and understand your own emotions. And that doesn't necessarily mean spilling them out all over the place. This needn't mean five years on an analyst's couch. While rumination on the past can be helpful if it leads to insight, and then action, rumination for the sake of rumination gets a bit pointless – even though it may be profitable for the analyst.

It's essential to have some insight into your emotions if you want to be irresistible. As we've described earlier, irresistible behaviour, as demonstrated by the great and good, is all about projecting the right emotion at the right time, and understanding the reactions of others. In an experiment, two volunteers described their moods at the outset, then sat quietly facing each other, while one was highly expressive and the other deadpan. At the end of the experiment they both described their moods again. Unsurprisingly, the more expressive person had been 'emotionally contagious' and changed the more deadpan person's mood. The great majority of us experience small changes in our own facial muscles when we look at someone else experiencing definite emotion.

Cultural influences may affect the expression of emotion, rather than the experiencing of it. When Japanese and American students watched scenes of appalling atrocities on television in the company of others, the Japanese were a lot less expressive of horror than the Americans. But when Japanese students watched these scenes alone, they expressed horror on their faces to the same extent that the Americans had.

It's definitely necessary, too, to be able to control your emotions – and demonstrate the right ones as appropriate – if you want to be successful in many roles. A researcher called Seligman found that among two groups of life insurance salespeople, optimists sold 29 percent more insurance in the first year of working than pessimists and a staggering 130 percent in the second year.

Being irresistible to others is very much about how we project and handle our emotions, and how we handle other people's. As I've mentioned before, the charismatic are able to project emotions that are highly contagious to many people – how they seem to feel inspires and motivates great numbers of we lesser mortals. But in every context of relationship building, whether it's concerned with finding Ms or Mr Right, or finding people who are on the same wavelength as you with whom to work and do business, emotional connection matters greatly. And, of course, we choose to continue or end relationships based on how we are feeling about them.

Emotional intelligence

Up until a few years ago, not much was written about emotions in the context of work and everyday life. But in the past five years or so, starting with Daniel Goleman's bestselling *Emotional Intelligence*, there has been a great surge of interest in the subject. This concept usually covers managing emotions – our own and other people's – and motivation. The surge in interest is probably to do with the fact that there has been a lot of progress in the understanding of the anatomy of emotion, and what exactly happens in the brain when we feel things. It could also be to do with the swelling ranks of women in the workplace, because women generally express emotion more readily than men. That's not, of course, to imply that men do not necessarily feel emotions as strongly. And a huge growth of interest in psychology might also explain why we've suddenly gone all touchy-feely: psychology is the fourth most popular subject for undergraduates to study, close behind law, computer science and business studies.

When I look at world events it certainly seems, at the time of writing, that globally we are in desperate need of more emotional intelligence. Think about it: school massacres, nail bombs, ethnic cleansing . . . what we need is a little insight into our emotions, and how to control them.

Understanding emotions

There are all sorts of situations where we might want to project irresistibility, and our emotions might sabotage this aim. An obvious example is a job interview where you want to appear confident and competent, but anxiety makes you appear very nervous and unsure of yourself. Or another instance might be in a personal relationship, where you really like someone but you don't know them very well, and something they do makes you feel angry or depressed – to the extent that you, or they, end the relationship. Or perhaps you've just met someone who could become a customer or a client, but you feel anxious about how they regard you, and so fail to make contact with them to further the relationship.

At work, especially, there are all sorts of un-spoken rules about projecting emotion. Most of the time we like ourselves and other people to appear to be and to feel reasonable and in control. We associate professionalism and good decision-making with these qualities. Certain emotional displays are welcome: warmth, enthusiasm, encouragement, passion and conviction. Certain others are taboo: grief, jealousy and hatred must be kept well beneath the surface. To help us to be irresistible in as wide a range of situations as possible, with a lot of different people, we can't have too much emotional understanding.

Sometimes we experience emotions without understanding why. Physical factors may play a part here, of course, including hormonal changes, illness and exhaustion, all of which affect our moods. It's likely, too, that there are genetic and conditioning influences on this. Where you've had a parent who experienced dramatic mood swings as part of a psychiatric disorder, then you may find yourself experiencing unpredictable and inexplicable moods yourself. In my twenties, I would find myself experiencing furious rage, an all-enveloping response that was outside of my conscious control and frightening to myself and others. Anyway, I had a lot of therapy and it went away, though I'm not sure whether this was down to the therapy or just something I grew out of. If you're experiencing a similar swamp of anger or depression, then do seek professional help.

We also experience milder emotions, without consciously understanding why. A sense of *déjà vu*, for instance, when visiting a new place, or a mild elation or slight sadness at inexplicable times. In *Emotional Intelligence* – essential reading if this subject interests you – Daniel Goleman describes how the *amygdala*, the part of the brain that responds initially with emotion, holds emotional impressions and memories which can short-circuit the thinking brain and respond separately from it, and before it.

There's a lot of debate around today about whether expressing emotions is good for us or not. Perhaps we're unwise to generalise about emotions anyway; while expressing some emotions may be helpful, expressing others may not. Certainly the experiences of breast-cancer sufferers who join support groups and, on average, enjoy 50 percent longer survival time would seem to suggest that sharing emotions in a supportive atmosphere is helpful.

But in *Emotional Intelligence*, Daniel Goleman describes how outbursts of anger pump up the emotional brain's arousal, leaving people feeling more angry, not less. It's almost like the outbursts are keeping the amygdala 'wired', so that a person becomes much more likely to blow a gasket again, soon. And these people are much more likely to have stress-related health problems, such as heart attacks.

So while it may be good for us to express our fear and anxiety, repeatedly getting angry doesn't seem to be very constructive.

When emotion overwhelms us, it becomes very difficult to think clearly and our concentration suffers. Let me reveal what happens when we literally let it all hang out. A recent survey showed that a large sample of women were so self-conscious and anxious about wearing bikinis that their concentration was measurably affected. The message here is: Girls, don't do it. Use common sense. Get yourself a nice covering one-piece instead, and a sarong too, if it helps.

The good news is there is a lot you can do if you are feeling emotional and you want to hide this, so that people remain under the illusion that you are calm and in control. Here we'll consider the most common sabotaging emotions: anger, depression and anxiety.

Believing you have the power

Above all, the sense that we can manage our emotions comes from the belief that we can change the state we are in. To do this, we need to by physically and mentally aware – to be alert and sensitive to both physical and psychological messages. If these awareness skills are rusty, then this may mean a few weeks of just checking in with yourself three or four times a day and asking yourself: How am I feeling now? What am I thinking? A word of advice here, though: don't expect anybody else to be interested in this; it's purely an exercise to improve your own self-awareness.

Distracting yourself

A few months ago I took a flight to the Channel Islands on business and, stuck for something to read, bought myself the latest Patricia Cornwell thriller. The chatty security officer in Jersey airport commented on my reading, marvelling at the number of passengers who went past him clutching Patricia Cornwell novels. For those of us who don't like flying, this is very sensible.

When individuals with similar levels of fear of flying sit on board a plane that is just about to take off, measurable physiological changes will occur. Pulse rates will increase, for one thing. These changes will be far less marked in someone who distracts themselves, through listening to music, watching a film or reading a gripping thriller. When the nervous flyer concentrates on the sound of the engines, the mood of the air crew, the captain's messages, the safety instructions, these physiological changes will be far more marked. Now I'm not suggesting that you ignore the safety guidelines, but if you concentrate singly on every aspect of information about airline safety you are much more likely to worry about it.

So, learning to consciously distract your attention when you are experiencing strong emotion can be very helpful. It's something most parents recognise as a good device for helping children who are upset – pointing out something interesting to look at, talking about something exciting that's coming up, or getting involved in a book or a video can help to distract and therefore soothe the troubled toddler.

If you're feeling upset in the office or nervous before an interview, distract yourself with a good book, a holiday brochure or some thoughts of your favourite form of relaxation.

When we learn to distract ourselves, we also learn to soothe ourselves. Distractions I find helpful include going mail-order shopping, going internet shopping, actually going-to-shops shopping, cooking, reading novels, e-mailing my mates and communing with nature while jogging or walking. All these activities alter arousal patterns in my brain and are pleasantly distracting.

Instantly irresistible

- When you find yourself obsessing about something, an injustice that's befallen you, or something you want that you can't have, then find something absorbing to distract you. Redecorate a room, plan a holiday, or take up a new interest.

Delaying gratification

When we learn to delay getting what we want, we have the key skill for making big deals at work. We learn to be patient and in any sort of deal-making this is the essence of success: to be able to wait until the terms are those that you want. So this use of emotional intelligence will make you more successful professionally.

In *Emotional Intelligence*, Daniel Goleman describes a study by psychologist Walter Mischel, where four-year-olds were given the choice between the instant gratification of getting one marshmallow, and the delayed gratification of running an errand first, and then getting two marshmallows. So the latter group understood delayed gratification. Twelve to fourteen years later, the groups were tracked down and Goleman comments:

> . . . the emotional and social differences between the grads – the preschool marshmallow grabbers and their gratification-delaying peers was dramatic. Those who had resisted temptation at four were now, as adolescents, more socially competent, personally effective, self-assertive and better able to cope with the frustrations of life. They were less likely to go to pieces, freeze or regress under stress, or become rattled and disorganised when pressurised; they embraced challenges and pursued them instead of giving up even in the face of difficulties; they were self-reliant and confident, trustworthy and dependable; and they took initiatives and plunged into projects. And more than a decade later – they were able to delay gratification.

The psychological portrait that emerged of the grabbers was much more troubled – they shied away from social contact, they were stubborn, indecisive, and easily upset by frustration.

As adults, of course, the extent to which we are capable of delaying gratification affects our physical and psychological health. Do we succumb to the short-term high of the cigarette, the double vodka or the Cadbury's Creme Egg, or do we take a longer-term perspective and consider the ventilator, the cirrhosis and the folds of fat?

I don't want to sound puritanical here – though in truth my genes are Baptist, so I'm naturally inclined in this direction. But certainly an understanding of how we are using short-term and long-term rewards can be very helpful, especially in the face of overwhelming emotion – because we often feel angry or frustrated because we can't get what we want immediately.

I reckon it's definitely possible to train yourself to get better at delaying gratification. Faced with a day's work, for instance, start with the most unpleasant task and then work through them in descending order of unpleasantness. If you've had a particularly unpleasant morning, then give yourself a small treat at lunchtime – a swim, an exercise class or a smoked salmon sandwich, for example. Truck on through the afternoon, and then reward yourself with whatever treat you fancy – rampant sex, a large gin, or my own particular and rather modest favourite: a read of the *Daily Mail*.

Consciously planning and giving yourself rewards is probably the most powerful way of focusing yourself, keeping motivated and avoiding the concentration collapse that comes from being overwhelmed by how you feel. So chop big tasks and challenges up into chunks and reward yourself fairly frequently as you work through those chunks. Many more people would write books, I'm sure, if they followed my scheme, and awarded themselves a bar of *premier cru* chocolate at the end of every chapter.

And when you really, really want something – marriage, a business deal, that latest Gucci bag – and it becomes problematic, avoid obsessing about it by taking a long-term view, and distracting yourself with other enjoyment.

Instantly irresistible

- When you are trying to stop yourself from doing something compulsively – eating, drinking or shouting at a colleague, for instance – fill out the moment between the stimulus to do it and your response. Stop yourself to think about long-term consequences of your action, and break the cycle between impulse and action. Extend this period of time, eventually aiming to delay the action altogether.

Detaching yourself

When we're in any situation, and we're appraising it, there are only four perspectives we can take:

- Our own perspective, seeing what's going on entirely from our own desires and feelings. This is a perspective people often take when they are feeling something very strongly.
- Another person's perspective, the 'you' point of view, where we empathise and put ourselves into another person's shoes and imagine how they might be thinking and feeling. This is an essential perspective to get a handle on for skilful negotiating of any description.
- 'Our' perspective – how all of us involved in the situation might be thinking, feeling and doing, including common goals, values and feelings that we all might share. Often people make assumptions that other people are more similar to them than they actually are, and are taken aback when they prove to be otherwise. Really getting a handle on a 'we' perspective can take quite a bit of research and time to establish.
- The perspective of a detached observer, or onlooker. This involves separating yourself from the situation, and viewing it as though you are an outsider. This can help to keep a sense of perspective about your situation, because your viewpoint creates distance, and also helps you to see the funny side of things.

As I was writing this book, I was involved in an odd and slightly disturbing incident. We moved to a beautiful listed building in Wales. Unbeknown to us, a week after our arrival, we found that the land next door had an appeal against planning permission turned down for a modern development of six flats. So we quickly had to muster our powers of protest and get organised for this enquiry, while unpacking cases, getting kids settled into nursery, getting phones connected and orientating ourselves to a very different place and lifestyle, to which we'd moved after decades of living in London.

I was put in touch with another local resident who was keen to protest at the enquiry. I'll call him JB. The council's planning department gave me his phone number, and when I called him, he suggested popping over to my new home to meet and discuss tactics, which we did. The following day we both attended the enquiry and I sat next to him.

The next morning I switched on the television news, to see that one JB was starting a trial for indecent assault committed at his home, very close to ours, and that he was a solicitor. He was convicted later in the week and it turned out that he had had previous convictions for assault.

On the day of discovery I felt quite shaken. But the following day, I was able to move to detached-observer position, to view the whole sequence of events from the perspective of an outsider. And, yes, there was something ironic about a middle-class mother moving from London, with fantasies of a wholesome, more innocent lifestyle, naïvely welcoming, as her first ally in her new home, an about-to-be-convicted attacker.

When we put ourselves into this role of detached

observer, it may help us to control feelings that are not being especially helpful to us.

Instantly irresistible

- When you're feeling confused about things that are going on in your life, it can be helpful to use this detached observer standpoint in the persona of your life manager, who views everything from a distance, and makes cool logical decisions about how best to manage it all.

Cooling anger

Anger is one of the emotions that people find most difficult to control, and it can have devastating consequences, if not handled well. In terms of your health – and relationship – the best approach to managing anger seems to be to express what's bothering you as early on as possible, rather than bottling it up and then exploding, or letting anger build so that you end up in an almost permanent choleric state, ready to let off at the drop of a comment.

As Daniel Goleman comments, 'An occasional display of hostility is not dangerous to health. The problem arises when hostility becomes so constant as to define an antagonistic personal style – one marked by repeated feelings of mistrust and cynicism and propensity to snide comments and put-downs, as well as more obvious bouts of temper and rage.'

Changes in the immune system that occur when a person is angry can cause increasing vulnerability to viral infections, heart problems, diabetes and asthma. So what can you do to control your anger? Here are some suggestions:

Instantly irresistible

- Catch those negative thoughts that start off an angry reaction. If you're starting to think: 'He's late again; he really doesn't have any regard for me,' nip that response in the bud and take the more philosophical 'He's late again, but I'll be really glad when he comes home'.
- Remember how we make attributions. Any dealings with others have three elements to them – your behaviour, their behaviour and situational factors. He may be late again because you are getting on his nerves generally, because he's under pressure and a symptom of this is that he can't manage his time properly, or Railtrack, London Underground or Virgin Trains could be the problem. Many of us tend to be generous in consideration of situational factors when we view our own transgressions, but consider others' shortcomings to be of their own making.
- Check that you are expressing what is making you angry early on. Assertiveness training suggests a three-part formula: specifying, revealing and predicting. Try something along the lines of: 'When you stay in the pub for two hours after

work (specifying), it makes me feel unwanted (revealing) and I will be moving out if you do it again (predicting).' Perfectly reasonable, don't you think?

- Take time out and remember that feeling angry is a high arousal state, so distract yourself through calming activities and conditions to change how you feel. Swimming in a quiet pool, meditating in a darkened room or reading the papers in a pleasant café can all help to appease the angry brain. Exercise helps, because our bodies react to the high activity by rebounding afterwards to a much lower state of arousal.

- Gestalt therapy suggests that acting out our impulses can be very therapeutic. So if you feel really mad at someone and you don't want to demonstrate this, punching a cushion and yelling at it can exorcise your unhelpful feelings.

Lifting depression

When you feel depressed you are in a low arousal state, and it can be very difficult to motivate yourself to do things. Depressed people aren't much fun to be around, and it's not usually a state that makes people irresistible. The guidelines here are for people who occasionally feel mildly depressed – and that includes a great number of us, I suspect – rather than people who are suffering from clinical depression. If you feel something stronger than a passing mood, then go and get an expert opinion to check that you are not suffering from clinical depression that may require treatment, whether pharmacological or psychological.

Instantly irresistible

- Vigorous exercise often helps a depressed mood, because it shifts a person from their low arousal state to a much higher one. And, of course, vigorous exercise produces feel-good chemicals in the body, called endorphins.
- Distract yourself from your depressed mood by going somewhere lively and stimulating, or taking up some interest that deserves those adjectives – line dancing, Indian cookery or abseiling.

Appeasing anxiety

In contrast, when we experience anxiety we are in a high arousal state and people who are chronic worriers will be beseiged by anxieties that seem to come from nowhere. Here's what to do.

Instantly irresistible

- Getting involved in activity that fully engages your attention may preclude the interruption of those nagging little concerns.
- Any relaxation methods may prove useful, such as exercises where you consciously scrunch up and

> relax bits of yourself, or you play mental imagery games and imagine yourself in paradise, soaking up the sun on a beach.
> • Anything that makes you feel better about yourself, and helps to relax you and give you a sense of well-being – aromatherapy massage, flotation tanks, great sex, a lovely meal prepared for you, listening to beautiful music – may allay anxiety, by making you feel that you are more able to cope.

Managing other people's emotions

We think and feel at the same time. Take the example of an examination, where you may be feeling quite nervous at the start, but you are able to think enough to start to answer the questions. Sometimes, though, it's easy to overlook the emotional aspects. Let's say at work you've spent a lot of time thinking up a new idea, which you want to convince others to support. In doing this you'll regard yourself as intellectually fencing with others, with little feeling involved. So you may think things like, 'I've got to go and convince my boss to invest in this project; he'll want good reasons and that's what I'll prepare.'

And, of course, ostensibly, your boss may be an extremely rational person and that will be the self-image that he wishes to perpetuate. But he may also be worried that if he invests in the wrong projects he may be judged harshly by his peers or that he won't make a go of his new role. These are emotional concerns and we all have them, whether we are aware of them or not. Even the one in six people who seem to be completely unemotional do experience the same physiological changes in emotion-generating circumstances as everyone else – it's just that connections for them between their emotional responses and conscious expression of them seem to be weaker.

Whenever we think about influencing people about anything, we need to ask ourselves how they might feel about the suggestion. Even though our audience might not be expressive about how they feel, that's not to say they are not feeling and concealing those feelings or experiencing them later on. And far more often than we realise, we may need to reassure people on some level – to reassure them perhaps that we'll be faithful and committed partners for life, to reassure them that the project in which we want them to invest will be successful, to reassure them that if they give us their business we will be excellent suppliers. Having that idea in the back of your mind – that people often need reassurance at some level – is a most useful one in using emotional intelligence. Learning to sound reassuringly authoritative, as I described in Chapter Six, is a most useful skill here.

Sharpening up your emotional intelligence

In the same way that our antennae about our own feelings can become insensitive through underuse, we may find it difficult to feel and display empathy if we haven't consciously been thinking about how others feel. We'll be likely to lose out, too, in any situations where strong feelings may be playing a part.

Instantly irresistible

- So, building on a previous exercise, you may find it helpful to ask yourself, three or four times a day, 'How's this person feeling about this?' And when you start to feel confident about your judgement, and if it is appropriate to ask them to check your judgement, ask 'Are you feeling happy about this' or 'Are you feeling doubtful about this?' When you're in doubt about how someone's feeling, because you suspect they don't want you to see how they're feeling, then asking them whether they feel the opposite to what you suspect, and noting their reaction, may get a more unguarded response.

- The best way of sharpening emotional intelligence is to get really good at listening and, while you're listening, to focus 100 percent on that person, and what they are really meaning. I realise that this is demandingly generous for many of us, but it's much more constructive behaviour for both parties than the sort of fake counselling 'touchy-feely' communication that goes on a lot of the time these days. You know the sort of thing: 'I hear what you say' and 'I know exactly how you feel.' Rubbish, how can anybody know that about anybody else? My view is that it's disingenuous to pretend that we are utterly generous towards one another and to ignore something that all of us have somewhere – an ego monster.

Letting ego monster out

Another way to use emotional intelligence is to be absolutely upfront and direct in your dealings with people, unless you feel it would hurt their feelings. It disarms people when we do this, and people are more easily influenced when they are disarmed. It also creates trust between you, and trust is a most important element in long-term relationship-building.

So if pressed be honest about what you can and can't do. Explain to people early on in interactions what you would like in a situation, if they seem confused about it. Don't think that having an ego makes you seem unattractive – it's disguising its desires that makes a person untrustworthy. Let people know about your goals and where you want to be going, and what you want to be getting out of a situation. This could involve being specific early on about how much money you need, or being upfront about where you want to be positioned in a company, or being very clear to people that you like to do business with people you regard as friends.

Establishing relationships

In the age of Bridget Jones, the papers are full of the plight of successful attractive thirty-somethings, both male and female, who find it difficult to get the relationship they want. The best advice I can give is to stop looking, 'cos desperation is the biggest turn-off ever. Having said that, there's no harm in deliberately involving yourself in activities that you as an individual especially like. Use a reputable dating agency if your social life needs a kick in the pants and hope for the best.

As for professional relationships, well, again, you have to put yourself about a bit. Let people know what you do and how you can help them. This goes for whether you're in full-time employment or are self-employed. In the latter case it's especially important. Do your own PR and publicise yourself by chatting to people at work-related social events, writing articles and giving talks. Run a lunchtime seminar on something that's of interest to everyone. Kate's a lawyer in a big city firm and did just this:

> I came to England from New Zealand a couple of years ago, and got a job here about eighteen months ago. To be truthful, I found English people generally rather reserved and difficult to get to know. One of my passions is yoga, so I thought that a way of getting to know more people in the firm, with similar interests to myself, and to keep

up my interest, would be to invite a recommended yoga teacher in one lunchtime a week. When I asked my senior partner about this he looked bemused, but the firm regards itself as progressive, so he gave me the go-ahead. The classes have turned out to be extremely popular, I've got myself known in the firm as a result and have made some really good chums.

Selling yourself into a relationship

In this country, people tend to be a bit sniffy about the idea of selling. It's as though it's something cheap and nasty, and if you're good at something, then people should mysteriously be able to sense that without you pushing it. But, interestingly enough, the word 'sell' comes from a Swedish word '*selzer*', meaning 'to serve'. If you regard yourself as serving others when you are selling yourself, a service or a product then it may become much easier for you. You are offering them something that could help them – and if they don't want it, well what the hell, someone else will.

Maintaining a relationship

All relationships – whether personal or professional – involve transactions and exchanges. He gives you confidence, his BMW to drive and an education into Italian cooking; you give him a feeling of security, bedspace in your flat and some dress sense. Your boss gives you support, a decent salary and lots of opportunities to take decisions; you give her loyalty, hard work and expertise on which she knows she can rely. When exchanges aren't equal – one partner giving a great deal more than the other – then relationships of any description are likely to sour. That's not to say, of course, that for some people the great buzz they get out of a relationship isn't a sense of martyrdom – the 'I've done this all for you' syndrome. The trouble is that the appreciation they get usually comes from sadists.

In my book, one of the most useful ways of analysing relationships is – funnily enough – through an approach called transactional analysis. You may be familiar with this idea; it was popular during the 1960s, and become well known through books like Eric Berne's *Games People Play*, and Thomas Harris' *I'm OK, You're OK*.

What transactional analysis says is that, as children, we learn behaviour patterns from adults around us and replicate these patterns. We can use analysis of these behaviour patterns to stop unhelpful rituals of communication, which can damage relationships. TA, as it's known by its afficionados, analyses these behaviour patterns in terms of being:

- adult – coolly logical and rational
- critical parent – disapproving and directing
- nurturing parent – caring and conciliatory

- free child – creative, spontaneous and mis-chievous
- adapted child – compliant and dominated

As adults, we will involve ourselves in transac-tions constantly in our dealings with one another. For example, you wake up in the morning and have an adult-to-adult conversation with your partner about the day ahead and arrangements after work. You jump the lights on the way to work in free-child mode and incur the wrath of a critical-parent fellow driver. You immediately take the role of nurturing parent when you get into the office – your team have experienced a lot of change recently and are generally unsettled. But you have to go and see the CEO, because your department's cocked up over something significant. You stick in adapted-child mode, because you know it works best with him. You have a meeting with your peers in which you are mostly adult, but when Hubert from Operations makes a few interesting comments, you go into free child, in order to flirt with him. On the way home, you drive past a new housing develop-ment that offends your sensibilities. You go into critical parent for a while, as you consider how the land should have been conserved as it was. When you get home, you have another adult-to-adult conversation with your partner about your day; you go into nurturing-parent mode as you sympathise with the rotten day he's had. Then, after the best part of a bottle of Merlot, you both go into free-child mode. And the rest can be left up to your imagination.

Avoiding relationship pitfalls

For psychological well-being, we need to be able to move around these states. Hence the cry of be-leaguered mothers at home everywhere for 'some adult company, please!' In relationships we may often set up patterns with others that are not very constructive, based on these states. You'll be familiar with some of these, I'm sure:

- The business provider who tends to be very demanding and pernickity, in critical-parent mode, with the supplier who goes into compliant, passive, adapted-child mode.
- The woman who wants to argue a point seri-ously, in an adult state, when her partner jokes and takes the mickey out of her – in free-child mode. She gets baited by him into moving into critical-parent mode.
- The man who acts helpless constantly in domestic affairs, in compliant-child mode, so that his partner – male or female – takes on the role of nurturing parent, constantly.
- The woman who takes on the role of critical parent with her partner, who is unreliable, while he takes on the role of free child and philanders as he likes, eventually leaving.
- The manager who, threatened by a subordinate's

creativity, constantly stifles their creative, free-child contributions, with a cool, logical, adult analysis of why their ideas wouldn't work.

There are many reasons why relationships go wrong, and they won't all be accounted for through transactional analysis. But the easiest thing to tackle about a relationship going wrong is usually the role we ourselves are playing in it. We can usually tackle this more easily than changing the other person's behaviour, or situational factors.

So, as a general guideline, if you find yourself playing a role too often in a relationship than is good for you, try and shift to a stance that is closer to the state that the other person is using, or one that is better able to handle their demands.

With a critical-parent supplier, or partner, then use an adult approach to coolly analyse what is wrong and how it can be put right. Use logic to focus on what can be done positively. With someone who goes into free child, which under-mines you when you want to be taken seriously, there is no point remaining serious. Go into free-child state, too. Joke and play around.

If, more often than you would like, you find your-self playing nurturing parent to a helpless partner or employee who's playing compliant child, then becoming a free child and joking and teasing with them, rather than looking after them and solving their problems, jerks them into responsible action. What's going on here is that through playing a different role, you stop rewarding the person for the role they are playing. Without their anticipated rewards, they may well change roles.

Some other games people play . . .

Transactional analysis describes some other games that people play with one another that can be destructive to relationships:

- **Kick me** This game is played by someone who would rather get negative attention than no attention at all – a very childlike response. So they constantly perform minor transgressions in order to get attention – forgetting things that matter to you, being late and performing behaviours they know to be irritating. The only way you can avoid being drawn into this game – and being forced to become a very critical parent – is to completely ignore the misdemeanours and make no comment.

- **Now I've got you, you son of a bitch** Yes, this quaint American-titled game is played by someone who knows you care greatly about something – like being very competent professionally, or a brilliant cook, or a generous friend. They will seek out, long-term, opportunities to undermine you, using what you care about most. So, at work they may point out minor mistakes; in the kitchen, small faults in your cuisine; in friendship, instances where you could have done more. If someone's playing this game on you, then you have to pretend that you do not care about their criticism. So shrug their comments off, with a 'pah, minor detail', if they attack your competence. Laugh and say, 'I was never great with eggs,' when they go for your omelette, or smile and explain that 'Sometimes you just have to say no', when they point out something you haven't done as a chum.

- **Yes but . . .** This is played by individuals who recognise that you regard yourself as a problem-solver. They aim to bait you into constantly solving their problems, while lining up more for you to solve. You can never win this game, because there are an infinite number of problems to be solved in the world. As a trainer, you get the odd individual on courses who likes to play this game. You can refuse to play with a 'Gosh, that's a terrible problem, good luck in solving it!' Again, you're avoiding playing the role you've been cast in.

- **The Karpmann triangle** This is a pernicious little game where people move around three roles: victim, rescuer and persecutor. Let's say someone has a problem at work and you counsel them about it. They are playing the victim here and you are helpfully rescuing them. But these counselling sessions become more frequent; indeed, virtually every time you see this individual, you end up giving them more of your time and energy. The roles have shifted here slightly, and you have become their victim, and they your persecutor. They are pulling your strings to get you to play counsellor. The only way out of this, again, is to stop playing the role, and to stop counselling.

Now if this is all making human beings sound terribly manipulative, this is not my aim. Very often healthy relationships thrive upon transactions – he plays nurturing parent and makes me feel confident about my work and I play free child and make him feel confident in bed. Or, in playing adult, she helps me see things more rationally about problems I have at work, while I make her feel more powerful about herself, through playing adapted child to her advice. And as our relationships – again, both personal and professional – change, the states we use with one another will change. A business relationship may develop from one where both parties tend to be in adult states, to one where they become friendly and relaxed enough with one another to express themselves as free children.

We can use knowledge of these states to increase our sensitivity to others and our appropriateness of response. We can help people feel better – and that, m'dears, is a big part of being irresistible.

Preserving your emotional energy

There's a lot of advice around about how to handle stress and how to eat and exercise for physical energy, but people rarely talk about emotional or psychological energy.

Relationship-making and -building takes a great deal of emotional energy and attention, and we only have so much of these to go around. That's probably a contributory factor to the fact that a lot of relationships go down the pan when children appear. I think we need to be as aware of our emotional and psychological reserves as our physical ones.

When colleagues or clients at work are being exceptionally demanding, then you may not have much in reserve for relationships at home. And vice versa. So be kind to yourself about this, and remember that our psychological reserves occasionally need recharging through self-indulgence, and through doing things that we really enjoy, creating that state called 'flow' (see page 230).

Understanding your emotions and being fairly certain that you can manage them is a great source of confidence – the sort of confidence that makes it possible for us to trust our reactions completely and know that we can give others our undivided attention. With this attention, we can help them manage their emotions, too – if we so choose. All this adds up to someone with a high degree of irresistibility.

9

Tactically Irresistible

You're reading this book because you want something. Maybe it's a promotion, or a guy who looks like Mel Gibson. Yes, I know, my age is showing! Or maybe you just want a few ideas to make you feel more confident about life and yourself in general.

So far I've given you lots of ideas for increasing your irresistibility in a variety of situations. I've covered many different approaches to ways of influencing other people. In this chapter, it's time to pull all the ideas together. Some of the ideas here have been mentioned earlier in the book; here I've made them highly context-specific. I'm going to look at five specific situations where most of us could do with some bolstering:

- getting our own way in arguments
- procuring friends and lovers
- dealing with incredibly difficult people
- achieving recognition at work
- becoming self-employed

Having read this chapter you can expect to be irresistibly argumentative, irresistibly seductive, irresistibly diplomatic, irresistibly significant and irresistibly self-sufficient. OK, so that may seem to you like a tall order and, of course, I don't know about the quality of the raw material that I'm working with. But one of the things I want to impress upon you in this chapter is a crucial concept: thinking big.

Just before we get into it, I want to say a word or two about tactics. Sometimes when I start talking tactics with people, their brows get furrowed and expressions of slight concern appear on their faces. Usually, they'll then express reservations about being underhanded or sly in their dealings with others. They want to be open and honest with people.

That's a very good sentiment, and holding it doesn't mean that you can't be tactical. Being tactical is just about thinking things through before you act, rather than acting impulsively, according to emotional responses you may not even be aware that you are experiencing. It's about thinking through how you will communicate, what you will say and how specific individuals are likely to respond to your messages. Being tactical is about considering crucial influences, such as the environment in which you're operating, the timing of when you communicate and how you do it. It's about considering nuance and subtlety, focussing your attention in order to roam in these shades of beige.

People often have reservations about ideas like using tactics, because they would like the world to be a very simple place. They would like all of us, as individuals, to follow the maxim 'What you see is what you get'. If this was the case with human beings all our dealings with one another would be plain sailing – as well as dramatically reducing professional opportunities for psychologists. Clearly, our dealings are not that straightforward. Wars start, relationships break down, parents fail, business deals collapse, crimes go undetected because, with human beings, what you see is *not* what you get.

Several years ago, there was a rumour that Saddam Hussein had several generals who had been given plastic surgery in order to look just like him. Quite plausible, in my view. Quite plausible, too, that a foreign power might pot a shot at one of these generals, celebrate their victory and, unbeknown to them, still have the real Saddam to contend with.

Just a couple of years later, a merger was proposed between two of the biggest pharmaceutical companies in the world – Glaxo Wellcome and SmithKline Beecham. The merger failed, it was widely reported, because the two personalities heading up these companies, Jan Leschley and Giordano, failed to get on with one another. Although on the surface negotiations between the two men seemed to be proceeding, their failure to get on ultimately thwarted this potentially massive merger.

At the time of writing, possibly Britain's most notorious rapist, with a suspected total of over a hundred rapes to his discredit, has just been convicted. He was caught because his brother saw a photofit of him on television and contacted the police. Looking at photos of Richard Baker in the newspapers, working as a DJ in Spain, and appearing handsome, fit and fun loving, it's easy to see how such a wholesome exterior could fool victims and police officers into a false sense of security.

No, what we see in one another is not what we get. We are all complex beings, the results of our unique genetic composition, and our conditioning and environment. Our bodies and minds are constantly changing, as is the world we occupy. If you adopt this philosophy – and I think you'd be wise to do so, says matron – then you will appreciate that a tactical approach to most things is the wisest. Because when people are complex and changing, and operating in a changing environment, then, try as we might, we may never be able to predict how they will behave, because we cannot know them that well. We can only guess at how they might respond in several different scenarios and that, of course, is the basis of tactical thinking.

Irresistibly argumentative

Ravinda's a lawyer:

> One of the things I'm really grateful for in my life is that my dad brought me up to enjoy arguing and

not to take it personally. Traditionally, Asian women are not brought up to stand their ground and argue, but my dad loved the cut and thrust of debate, and as soon as we were old enough, my brothers and myself would sit around with him in the evening, and he would discuss political and religious issues with us. Sometimes he would be deliberately provocative and take up an extreme position, to wind us up and to teach us how to cope with that. I never take disagreement as being personal, and I sometimes have to be careful with people who do, because when I start to challenge and counter, they immediately back down. It's usually more a personal than professional concern, as you can imagine.

It's very useful to be able to take up a position of detachment when arguing, so that you do not perceive yourself to be and then feel under attack personally. Better to regard it as a game of brinkmanship – with a variety of tactics at your disposal. I love a good argument. The trouble is, I'm psychopathic about winning and will pull every dirty trick in the book in order to do so. My nearest and dearest now, wisely, walks away.

And that's probably the first thing to decide about arguing. Is it worth it? There's no point expending energy on something that's not important to you, or on a minor detail in your life. Even if the other person has baited you so that you feel incensed, if it's 'small stuff' as Richard Carlson calls it in his *Don't Sweat the Small Stuff*, then leave it. And when you feel mad at the other person, just take a stroll in the park, go down the pub, or go shopping and take calming time out.

Once you've decided that something is worth fighting for then here are some guidelines to make your argument irresistible.

When you've not been conditioned to view disagreement and arguing your case as appropriate behaviour, you may have to play mental games to create a suitable and sustaining image for yourself. So stage one of this arguing business is:

Viewing yourself as a warrior princess/prince or hunter

No, I haven't gone completely potty here and I'm not just about to go off running barefoot with the wolves. But if viewing yourself as a person who relishes and seeks victory is outside your history, it is helpful to fantasise about yourself as some sort of glorious fighter, aiming at some glorious goal. This fantasising is helpful in all sorts of contexts. One fantasy I particularly enjoy is that of myself as earth mother, fighting for the good of my future generation, as I struggle with my buggy on the tube taking the kids to the museum.

Construct your argument pithily

It's best to state upfront what you're asking for. And, if it's shocking, give them a moment or two to recover, if the shock will prevent them hearing what you're saying. If time allows, and you do want to make a huge request, you might be better off asking for a bite-size chunk first, which will make your subsequent requests more palatable.

Show the process you've gone through in coming to your request. We've talked about this in Chapter Five. What you're doing here is story-telling, our most powerful means of communicating with one another. Have a clear through-line in your argument, which takes your opponent stage by stage through your case. But avoid minor detail and side-tracking by asking yourself, What is the minimum they must know here? Be ready to add further detail when challenged.

Be absolutely clear what's in it for them

There is no point in being disingenuous about this. If you threaten people with the idea that they will lose something – and remember, loss can be a very powerful motivator – then be absolutely explicit and upfront about this. And also be absolutely clear about what it is, in your view, they will gain.

Use the big picture and overriding principles

We are much more likely to allow ourselves to be persuaded to do things when we think they are significant in the great scheme of things, and when we think we are following sound principles. Danny just fought successfully against a development on adjoining land where he lives:

When I went to the inquiry, I was struck by the fact that the inspector, appointed by the government to adjudicate in this instance, seemed like a very decent sort of person. So I argued on the principle that this decision was about conservation and quality of life versus property developer's profits. The inspector did seem to note this and ruled in our favour.

Most of us like to feel we are decent sorts of people.

Give them your wholly focussed attention

Probably the most important tactic in presenting an irresistible argument is to make the person you are arguing with feel that they are very important and that their response to your ideas has been considered. Sometimes this may mean it's tactically wise to present an argument about which you are totally convinced in a more halting way than you would naturally. This means that you may need to sprinkle your case, with checks on how your audience is receiving it, with 'I don't know what you think about that', 'You might think it would work well this way; it would be good to hear your views' or 'What do you think of what I've said so far?' The aim of these checks is to create a conciliatory effect, to show your listeners that you have made no assumptions about their receptivity. You are wooing them here and it's a very softly, softly approach.

Ask them to interrupt, to respond, to ask you

questions and to express their concerns. Getting involved is a way of starting commitment, and we know from the law of consistency that once people start getting involved they are more likely to strengthen that involvement.

When your audience makes points, or asks questions, listen intently and have the confidence to ask questions that are subsequent to these, rather than pursuing your own agenda, regardless of their concerns.

Clarify and repeat your key request

You can deal with any sort of distraction, and what may seem to you to be irrelevant concerns, if you are absolutely clear about your key request. Often, your audience may throw you off course by chatting about other things, or going off on a tangent. If you've got your request down to one incisive plea – 'My department's asking for two million pounds' – then you can repeat this and use it to bring people back on track. When people aren't listening very well, this 'broken CD' technique can help get your message through.

Be passionate, and stay calm

Depending on who you are trying to convince about something, you must decide on how passionate or cool you play it. Generally speaking, creative types are more likely to be turned on by passion, while bank managers, lawyers and accountants may find it rather embarrassing, and prefer a much cooler approach. But let's say you're trying to get some venture capital, and on paper you know your business looks as solid as a competitor. A display of your commitment to and belief in your business may well tip the decision in your favour, however coldly rational the venture capitalists view themselves.

Pause for reservations

When people are expressing their concerns about your proposal, ditch the urge to rush in and counter their concerns. Give them plenty of opportunity to have their say, and pause before you respond, giving them airtime to say more if they wish. When people are given lots of space like this, they are much more likely to come to what's really bothering them about the proposal. Now I'm not suggesting that you use interminable pauses in the way that some therapists do, but given space we are much more likely to articulate what's really bothering us.

Walk away when it's not working

This is about knowing when to quit, and also keeping a balance on the emotional capital you are investing in something. If you're not getting anywhere, then you may be better off withdrawing and regrouping. Don't get so obsessed with wanting something to the exclusion of everything else. Nothing in life is that important and remember that desperation is the biggest turn-off.

And now I'd like you to walk away with me, please. Come and think about how we can become:

Irresistibly seductive

Having been married to the same bloke for twenty years – we married just after I left university, just so you don't think I'm *that* old – hardly qualifies me as an expert on irresistible seduction from personal experience. But as a psychologist with a special interest in how we communicate and influence one another, I think I can venture a few opinions here:

Don't take yourself too seriously

Yes, it's important to have things about which you care deeply and feel passion and commitment. But don't let one of these be your fragile ego, or you'll be a fun-free zone. And being seductively irresistible is all about having fun.

Why is it that sometimes the plainest people attract the most eligible partners? The fun factor, that's what. They get their partners giggling helplessly and then roll them into bed. Having a laugh is a fantastic aphrodisiac – we lose our inhibitions and produce endorphins, the feel-good hormones that boost self-esteem. So when you amuse someone into becoming a conquest, you give them an experience that is highly addictive. Chances are, they'll be back for more.

Fun is a great antidote to desperation, too. So if you're worrying desperately about your single status or your biological clock, get out there and have some fun. Do something that's completely outside your day-to-day life – maybe white-water rafting, trampolining, a murder-mystery weekend or seeing a kids' show. Let yourself lighten up.

Give people a get-out

There's a lot of guesswork involved in seduction. Sometimes people go along with suggestions because they don't want to hurt another person's feelings by rejecting them. I don't have to tell you, I'm sure, that this is a dodgy basis for a relationship because it's fundamentally dishonest.

It's much wiser to seduce people into doing things because they really want to do them. Just phrasing a suggestion so that it offers a get-out indicates to people that they have this option. So rather than, 'I thought you might possibly like to come and see that film next week?' followed by a dramatic intake of breath where you wait for the response, use an 'I know you're really busy at work at the moment, so you may not have the time, but I'm going to see that film next week, if you fancy it'.

When in doubt be upfront

If you really don't know where you are with someone, perhaps they're playing hard to get, or have a 'treat 'em mean and keep 'em keen' philosophy. Be upfront with them – you don't want to waste your valuable time and energy on a game-player. Miranda told me this story:

> I'd been seriously involved with someone for seven years, and then it all fell apart really badly, as we realised we wanted very different things in life. I met Paul a few months later, and he was everything my parents always wanted for me – unlike my previous boyfriend. I immediately became very keen on him, but wasn't at all sure about his feelings towards me. So on our third date, after three glasses of wine, I blurted out that I liked him very much, and would like to develop our relationship. What did he think? I was aghast when he said that he'd really like to be friends with me, but no more. On reflection, though, his honesty was really helpful and prevented me from deluding myself. We've stayed friends and I've since met a guy with whom I'm having a really great relationship. And, by the way, he wouldn't be my parents' choice, which is probably a recommendation.

This goes for sex, too. Consideration and honesty are great turn-ons here. Ask people what they would like, tell them what you would like and what your intentions are, and ask them whether they would like you to perform your intentions. Ignore this advice if masochism is your big turn-on.

Use compelling behaviour

Just to recap here, this involves giving the other person your complete and utter attention. Remember that those seducers, Kennedy and Clinton, move their eyes from eye to eye of the person to whom they are talking, creating the effect that they really care about what makes the other person tick. And use the warm olive oil approach to voice production, speaking in a confiding way, to create an auditory cuddle.

Compliment and appreciate the other person

Let the other person know directly what it is you appreciate and value about them, and when they've done things that you admire or please you. Endorse their self-image by complimenting them particularly on things you know they especially value. This isn't creepy, it's just using psychological insight to boost others. In my view, it's a generous act.

Irresistibly diplomatic

When people seem to be very difficult and impossible to please, they can undermine your confidence, making you feel powerless. You may even feel undermined to the extent that you feel there's no point in trying to influence anything or anybody. Here are some tactics for dealing with these incredibly difficult people.

Remember their fear

It's a cliché, but we do unto others as we have been done unto and as we do unto ourselves. So if someone is giving you a hard time, it'll be because they've been on the receiving end of this treatment themselves. Otherwise, how would they know that it was effective and hurtful? Often, too, people are awkward and difficult because deep down they are fearful of something – like other people dominating them, or not being taken seriously.

These people often think that they are 'testing' others with qualities that they respect as dear to their self-image. Pretty incredibly, Margaret Thatcher was said to want John Major to succeed her because he stood up to her in Cabinet. She respected assertive behaviour and he showed it.

And that they want stroking

So at some level very difficult people often want reassurance, and to be told that everything will be OK. You will find it helpful to work out the pay-off for their awkward behaviour. Are they just plain sadistic and get off on seeing others crumble? Or do you suspect they are awkward to look good – as they see it – in front of their peers? Or are they being awkward because belittling others makes them feel relatively more important? If you withdraw the pay-off for their awkward behaviour, then you take away the carrot that makes them behave in the way they do. So this may involve acting tough when you feel like crumbling, engaging with their peers as you're on the receiving end of their cruelty, and just not allowing yourself to be belittled by their treatment.

People also need reassurance that they are not what they most fear being. This means that we are terrified of being found out to be lacking in a quality that is very dear to us. Human beings get obsessed with some common qualities: being highly competent, being in control, being individualistic and being acceptable. You can often tell what people fear most by their outward behaviour:

Ben is a multi-million-pound business success, a self-made man who has built up his own company and become enormously successful in his industry. He is always absolutely immaculately dressed, the muscles in his body are pumped every morning for a couple of hours, and in meetings and social events, he will fiddle around constantly, picking bits of fluff off carpets, arranging everything on the table so it's perfectly in order, adjusting his clothes and appearance so that they gleam with absolute perfection.

Yes, you guessed it, Ben is a complete and utter control freak, and when he has to go into situations where he momentarily feels out of control, like large conferences where he's a guest speaker or among people with whom he's not familiar, he often falls apart for a moment and commits enormous gaffes by behaving really inappropriately.

Check it's not a status thing
Much earlier in this book, we talked about personal construct psychology and how we interpret everything through constructs. If we've got a hyper-sensitive superior/inferior construct through

which we interpret the actions of nominally higher-status people, then we may need to redress this, by replacing this superior/inferior filter with one that says, 'What have I got in common with these people?' and 'How am I different?'

In situations where you feel in awe of people you believe to be difficult, keep asking yourself that question: 'What have we got in common here, and how are we different?'

Bear in mind, too, that sometimes people are difficult because they may suspect that you are making assumptions about common goals they do not consider themselves to share with you. So being upfront about differences between you may be a helpful tactic.

Don't make assumptions about their goals

If you're guessing what they want and are hoping to achieve, it's wise to check this guess with them, or ask them directly what it is they are aiming for.

When you remain unclear about their agenda, keep asking them for reasons for their views. There's a formula that says that if someone's bluffing and you ask them 'why' five times, then you will almost certainly get to their real agenda. While 'why' asked five times in a row might irritate a touchy individual, there are various ways of pursuing this line of enquiry. Use phrases like, 'I'd like to know the thinking behind that', 'What led up to you coming to this conclusion', or 'May I ask the reasons for that?'

Use naïvety to disarm them

When a difficult person is expecting to do battle, they will often expect you to try to impose your will over theirs. And supremacy of will is very tied up with status, looking good and not showing your vulnerability. The risk of loss of face is something that exacerbates a great deal of conflict, because looking good is more important to the individual than getting an effective outcome in negotiation with the other person.

So you can effectively disarm a difficult person who has this expectation by expressing naïvety about something, or asking them for advice or information. You will reframe their role then, from combatant to advisor or mentor.

And when the chips are down, ask again for direction

The most effective technique customer-care training teaches people is to ask the complainant what they would like to have done about the problem. So, if you're mad as hell with BT, and you phone up to have a massive moan, and the situation permits it, the customer-care person may well say 'And what would you like us to do to help put this right?'

Apply this idea with difficult people if they're criticising or attacking you. Ask them 'What do I have to do to put this right?' In doing this, you are showing that your aim is constructive and that you

are highly receptive to their ideas about a solution.
It's an open, positive approach.

Deflect personal attacks

The difficult person's reputation may precede them
and make us hyper-sensitive to their behaviour, so
that we get more sensitive than we need to be to
their responses. Or they may deliberately attack
others and belittle them personally, because it
makes them feel superior and better.

In either case, if you sense that the subject matter
does seem to be turning into a personal attack on
you, move on to talk more about features of the
situation. This depersonalises things. If your
pursuer is relentless, you may decide to tackle them
with an 'I'm interpreting this as a personal attack;
please could you tell me why you are doing this?'
Let them blow and then use the 'What do I have to
do to put this right?' approach.

Acknowledge their feelings and say sorry

Though you may feel embarrassed or uncomfortable with their behaviour, it's important to let them
know that you have received their criticism. For
instance, there's nothing more galling to the
incensed director than to be told by a chirpy
manager, 'Yes, well, the reasons we did it were . . .'
It's far better that the manager lets the director
know that her feelings have been received with an
'I can see you're very concerned about it'. Weather

the storm if the director blows at this point, and when she's calmed down, come in with your reasons.

To mollify feelings, you have to acknowledge them. If you pretend they don't exist, they won't go away. They will fester, and erupt horribly at a later date.

Sometimes, macho business books advise that you should never say sorry. What baloney. We all cock up and we all need to say sorry at times. It shows consideration to others to do so. If an apology's necessary, then give it – it's an acknowledgement of your humanity.

Let people say no; stay on the sidelines

Giving difficult people choice is one of the best tactics for handling them. I often have to train people who are highly sceptical about my subject. So I frame my training session as a description of the sort of work I do with people like prime ministers and suggest that participants *may* find the content useful in a professional or even a personal context. I also suggest that if they don't want to join in with any of the exercises, then they don't need to. And guess what usually happens – yes, they all listen avidly and join in all the exercises, largely because they've been given the choice whether or not to do so.

Difficult people are much more likely to say 'yes' when you've given them a clear indication that they can say 'no'.

Time your interjections appropriately
Alex runs a conference production company:

> One of our clients was arranging a conference which was very important to the company, as there was a change of chief executive, dissent among the existing directors, and the workforce was demotivated. The aim of the conference was to establish stability and make people feel a bit more motivated. They asked me to sit in on a board meeting to talk about arrangements. I was rather awestruck and, as there were some very tetchy difficult characters among the directors, the atmosphere was highly charged.
>
> But, just before they came to talk about the conference arrangements, they started to talk about the main messages. I knew from experience that they were at risk of getting this badly wrong. Though it wasn't really my moment to contribute, I felt I had to blurt out and say something or the conference would not achieve its goals. So with a 'Would you mind if I chipped in please?' I proceeded to speak from my experience. They all listened, and altered their message as a result.
>
> After I'd said my bit, and we'd finished on the subject of the conference, another controversial item was raised. The discussion got stuck, and I was hugely flattered when the MD said, 'Alex, we realise you're not expert on this, but as an outsider, what's your view?' I left feeling pretty pleased with myself.

When handling difficult people, and if you feel strongly about an issue they need to hear, go ahead and speak. When they're feeling strongly about something, let them express those feelings before replying.

Let them view you as an archetype

Years ago, I worked with someone who defied easy categorisation. She was glamorous, brittle and tough – a type I think marketeers define as an 'executive tart'. In contrast, I know I've always come over as a jolly, slightly bolshie, mumsy type. Yes, sad but true.

She was every bit my equal when it came to running workshops, but we noticed that with one of our clients in particular, she seemed to have difficulties creating a rapport. This client employed a lot of ex-army officers – middle-class, conservative males, who found it much easier to relate to mummy-ish me than 'top-totty' type her.

All people, and especially difficult ones, who will always be confused at some level in order to be difficult, may find it easier to relate to you if you are, in some ways, an easily recognisable archetype.

Just think of how Margaret Thatcher used Nanny as one.

Walk away and live to fight another day

There are sadistic bullies in the world and if you have to handle one of these frequently, your attention and energy might be better employed elsewhere. I'm genuinely sorry for you if you have one of these as your direct boss, and if this is the case, you may well be better off in the long term taking a sideways move in order to progress upwards. When a nasty boss is hell-bent on blocking your progress, then you will need to sidestep them. Life is too short for you to allow people like this to mean that much to you.

Phew. That's difficult people done with. Now let's move on to how we can get the recognition we deserve at work.

Irresistibly significant

Getting recognition at work is often *not* about being great at your job – you need to be *good enough* at it – it's about being great at publicising how great you are at your job. In other words, doing yourself great PR.

Positioning yourself – literally

In the last government, there was a very tall, ambitious, status-conscious minister who held high office – a male. There was also a very small and feisty female minister, who frequently had to attend meetings with this other minister. The tall male minister would seat himself in a grand seat behind a grand desk. His visitor would be seated on a small chair, on the other side.

At the first meeting these ministers held together, the small female minister asked if she might possibly change something about the room arrangement, if the grand minister did not mind. He was bemused, but agreed. In came a chair and a desk for her, with the chair at least as lofty as the one he sat on. Believe it or not, this is a true story and I hope you're all cheering for that small feisty female.

Where we position ourselves will indicate to others the extent to which we are deserving of significance. At the office drinks 'do', for instance, do you hug the parameter of the room, fairly close to the door, or do you sweep into the centre of the room where you know all the action will be?

In meetings, either head of the table is the most powerful position. Next best bet, if you want to hold influence there, is to position yourself in the middle of one of the long sides. The corner positions will be weakest.

When you're trying to influence a meeting with confederates, it's wise to get them dotted around the group, which gives them most infiltration across the territory and the widest scope to clock people's responses. And if this all sounds very Machiavellian, well it is, and these days, if we're going to get anywhere, we need to be.

Understanding your power

Power's a dirty word at work and, in my experience, people get far more embarrassed about talking about power than they do talking about sex or money. But your power is a most precious resource, and if you want more recognition at work, then you have to have worked out what it is others will want you for. Here are some different types of power.

• **Expert power** – Heads of IT, for instance, usually have a lot of this at their disposal. Many of us are usually and quite wisely sceptical of people who claim to be experts. It seems like half the working population today hold the job title 'consultant'. When it's expert power you're selling, aiming for solid qualifications and a good practical track record giving evidence of your expertise are worth going for.

Just to remind you, too: expertise in a narrow specialist area, with an unusual combination of subjects, can become very valuable if it fits in with current trends.

• **Resource power** – Finance directors always have this, unless the company's on its last legs. Your resources may be much less tangible than this – perhaps you can claim access to government ministers, a long list of famous connections, knowledge you have about somebody's vulnerabilities, or about their true character. Where your resources are of a discretionary nature, timing will be everything in using them to raise your profile.

Resource power is used as a reward or a threat. When you get a promotion, you'll let the directors meet all your rich and famous friends. If you don't, then they'll stop being customers.

• **Legitimate power** – This means title power, like CEO, MD or operations manager. People who overuse titles often have little belief in other forms of power they might possess. It should only be used very rarely, when nothing else is available: 'I'm asking you to do this because I am the chief executive, that's why.'

When legitimate power is used to coerce people, it breeds resentment.

• **Personal power** – We're back to the subject of charisma, and that is really what much of this book is about – our beliefs and our abilities to influence others. I believe this form of power can be developed dramatically, which is a reason why I wrote this book. When we use our personal power effectively, we engage people's hearts and their imaginations. We sense clearly how they will feel about things, and identify common ground and visions that will inspire them.

To become irresistibly significant you need to do a quick audit of your power: do you need to bolster it up anywhere and are you aware of its limitations?

Getting your PR campaign going

This can be great fun – viewing yourself as a product that you are going to market to the heights of success. The first thing to do is to work out, in a word or two, what you want to be known for. Are you an innovative manager, super-caring teacher, entertaining accountant (yes, it's possible) or a dynamic lawyer?

The next step is to work out how you start to showcase yourself as this. Conferences, articles, interdepartmental meetings, industry-related exhibitions and networking clubs all provide opportunities. Remember the power of stories – what's your special story, and how can you communicate it to others? There are some stories that always travel well: the first or last ever, local girl/boy makes good, tremendous success or failure, and an interesting innovation.

In an organisation of any description, you need to target your boss's boss. They should somehow know all about what you're up to, so that they consider you to be a great deputy when your boss is indisposed. And when you're involved in something especially interesting, memo everyone so they know, especially your boss's boss – all in the name of good communication, of course.

Irresistibly self-sufficient

I've always been self-employed and I wouldn't change this situation for the world, especially with two children. But I enjoy my own company probably more than many people, and I rarely find it difficult to motivate myself. These inclinations are important to consider if you're thinking of branching out on a solo basis.

I'd suggest you *do more than one thing*. Cross activities, cross industries, or both. That way, you protect yourself against boredom and recession in particular markets. Let's say you want to provide

IT consultancy to small businesses, then I would do both consultancy and training and aim to get some charity or public-sector clients, too.

When you're working from home, *physically compartmentalise your work area*, even if it's only a screen across the corner of the room. This will help you mentally compartmentalise it, too. Many people who work from home don't have much problem getting down to work – it's switching off that's the problem. Having always worked from home in four different houses, I would say that having a distinctive area of the house – an annexe, a floor or an attic that is dedicated to work, and clearly separated from the kids' area – works well. This will minimise the likelihood of your printer needing to be fixed because it's jammed with Duplo, for instance.

As for getting business, then *read Tom Lambert's book* High Income Consulting, which has ideas for all sorts of ways to get business for all sorts of people. And never underestimate your instincts. When I first started my training business I set up an open course called 'Voice Training for Trainers', aimed at trainers in large organisations. My friends thought I was barmy – who would want such an obscure course? But this course became one of our most popular and rarely needed any marketing effort.

Remember that the fully employed often have fantasies about the self-employed life, and that it is the fully employed who will be giving you business. These fantasies include 'It's the life of Riley', 'very little work, piles of money', 'usually bullshitters' and 'irresponsible and slippery'. You may have to make definite efforts to counter these impressions.

In my experience, you increase your irresistibility as a self-employed person if you *let people know how busy you are*, if you *tell them your fees are expensive*, if you *are absolutely honest about what you can and can't do*. The latter is especially important because it's very tempting when you start out and are desperately keen to get business to stretch the boundaries of what you can and can't deliver. That doesn't mean avoiding accepting challenges. Please do, but do them safe in the knowledge that you have the necessary core skills, if not the experience.

Be upfront and clear about money and learn to enjoy talking about it. Let your clients and customers know absolutely everything that they will get for your fees.

One of the most enriching parts of my life has been my twenty years of self-employment. I've learned loads, and met many really interesting people. I've shaped my work so that I really, really love most of what I do. But I've realised, too, that it only suits certain personalities – those with low needs for stability, predictability and social satisfaction at work. Should you choose to take this route, I wish you the very best of luck. Here's to your self-sufficiency.

So that's Chapter Nine: how to be irresistibly argumentative, irresistibly seductive, irresistibly diplomatic, irresistibly significant and irresistibly self-sufficient. Loads of ideas, but what you need to do now is act. So please listen to matron and before proceeding to read the grand finale, do something that will shove you in the irresistible direction you desire. Go for it.

10

Love, Work and Staying Irresistible

Despite being somewhat out of fashion at the moment in psycho circles, Dr Freud knew a thing or two. And he contended that the two most important matters in our lives were how we loved and how we worked. I reckon he had a point. When people are asked about 'defining moments' in their lives – great turning points that they remember well – the two most cited memories are first loves and first jobs.

So I thought a fitting end to *Irresistibility* would be to consider how we can feel irresistible in love and at work over our entire lifetimes. Much of this chapter will be about getting older and how we adjust to change. I'll start by looking at some general ideas about getting older, and then look at how to keep feeling irresistible in our relationships as we get older. I'll move on to look at how to handle these relationships to feel irresistible in both love and work. Finally, I'll look at ideas about how to stay feeling irresistible at work, as we grow older.

Now you're probably thinking, 'Oh, it's the having it all debate,' which has been going on for years, since women *en masse* started going back to work. You'd be right. I believe strongly it is possible to have it all, whether you are a woman or a man, but the timing of what you have and when is crucial. And so is how you negotiate with your nearest and dearest supporters about who gets what, and when.

You'll possibly notice that I am determinedly avoiding the word 'ageing' in all this description, because it sounds so depressing. I'm in my early forties. Now from all that I read, this is the time of life when one has to face up to getting older, so my antipathy to the 'ageing' word may be highly subjective. All you younger readers, for whom I feel not a shard of envy, please bear with me. You'll get here one day.

Getting older irresistibly

'Fifty is the new forty!' declared Chrissy Hynde, lead singer of the Pretenders. At the time of writing Mick Jagger is touring with the Rolling Stones – average age around about fifty-five. Marianne Faithfull, Mick's ex, meanwhile, has just appeared in the *Times* magazine, in her underwear, to show how marvellous it is being fifty. Certainly this lot of 1960s survivors don't seem to have many problems believing that they remain irresistible while getting older.

A few years ago, 'stage theories' of careers were popular among psychologists. These prescribed different activities people were meant to do at different times in their lives. So, for instance, one's twenties would be a time for exploration, and settling down, with possibly some reproduction thrown in. One's thirties a time for consolidation and perhaps a bit more reproduction. One's forties a time for a mid-life crisis, and saying goodbye to the kids. One's fifties were a time for winding down, and worrying about retirement. All this sounds dismally predictable and fortunately less relevant for a lot of us today.

These days, we have far greater choice over what we do when. A couple of years ago, Elizabeth Buttle, a West Walian farmer, gave birth to her second child when she was sixty-one. Mary Wesley, the best-selling novelist, started her writing career in her late sixties. At sixty-eight, Pierre Gruneberg is a celebrity coach, teaching the great and good to swim in the summer in Cap-Ferrat, and teaching them to ski, in the winter, in Courcheval.

Medical developments and improvements in our quality of life mean that, in the Western world at least, we are all living longer and better. It is predicted that in the year 2020, over half of the European population will be over sixty. There are going to be a lot of us oldies around, and our oldie pounds or ecus will mean all sorts of business opportunities for drug companies, pension companies, nursing-home providers and incontinence-pad manufacturers.

At least we'll have security in numbers.

Lifetracking

Even though many of us will contradict the norms of stage theories, William Bridges, in his excellent book, *Transitions*, suggests that over a lifetime there is a journey we make as we develop into fully mature adults. This is primarily an emotional journey, as we learn from our experience and develop our confidence.

As children, in our teens and early twenties, we are in a state of dependence, working towards independence. So in our twenties many of us are almost acting as pretend adults, trying out roles and relationships both in love and work. (You possibly know some 45-year-olds who've got stuck in this stage. I certainly do.) Then, in our thirties, we move into adulthood proper, getting established in our relationships and careers. This is where we experience full independence. In our forties we may need to confront our 'nevers' – face facts that we may never be prime minister, or never raise three children and live in a cottage in the country, or never become a multi-millionaire. And if we are lucky, we will move from independence to a sense of interdependence, with the understanding that everyone is a separate and distinctive individual but that co-existing with others, and appreciating our dependency on one another, is greatly fulfilling.

This doesn't mean that forty-somethings inevitably experience mid-life crises. In terms of our aspirations, a crisis can occur any time we realise that what we wanted and expected is wildly out of kilter with what we've got. But it does mean that our aspirations may change as we approach the second half of life and burning ambition may be replaced by something mellower and less self-centred.

Research into highly successful career women in the USA showed that a very large number of them had a 'career moratorium' around about forty. This meant that in some instances they decided to have children, or developed consuming outside interests – new hobbies, skills or charity work – or threw themselves into their social lives and making new relationships. While the great majority of them continued to work, they shifted their main focus of attention away from work for a while, in order to develop in other areas. The research demonstrated a shift of direction from the single-minded striving associated with independent ambition, to a more balanced, broader approach to life.

A crisis of image

Scarily, the chronology of our lives may very often imitate that of our parents, without our realising it. John, an IT director, said:

Last year, we decided to move out to the country, having lived in the city all our married lives – about fifteen years in total. We wanted to move for the quality of life and because our eldest daughter was about to start secondary school and we wanted her to go to a really good one. I was just talking to my father about it, and he mentioned that, of course, I was about the age he was when they moved from the country to the city. This struck me as highly significant even though the nature of the moves were in reverse. It was as though, unconsciously, I was following some patterns based on his life.

Images we have of ourselves, too, may be based on our parents – consciously or unconsciously imitating them or reacting against them. We might expect, for instance, that someone who as a child holds a powerful image of her mother as a glamorous and alluring woman could herself grow up into an aspiring femme fatale. Trouble will arise for this individual when she persists in viewing and conducting herself as a femme fatale, when the rest of the world is viewing her as a washed-out old crone.

Now we've got to get real here. Our media glorifies images of the young, the slim and the beautiful. Past a certain age, as Dorothy Rowe points out in *Time On Our Side*, we become invisible to lots of members of the public. She cites an instance of waiting in a hotel reception to get a deposit box, while a dashing young airline pilot approaches the same receptionist, expecting to get immediate attention in front of the sixty-something invisible lady she represents. When you're not obviously bedable, bankable or notable to others, you are much likely to be ignored by a lot of people. And that's what happens to a lot of us as we get older.

When there is a clash between your self-image and the expectations society holds of you, there may be difficulties. You may be ridiculed for wind-surfing at seventy-five or berated by your family for choosing not to have children by the time you're thirty-eight. You may be patronised and over-looked because you do not appear to be a mover and shaker. But, so what? None of us have anything to prove at any age; we don't have to know where we're at at forty, or be stunningly sexy at fifty. We just have to seek out other people who appreciate and accept us for who we are.

Getting older is especially difficult for those of us who define ourselves very much through our sexuality. The press revel in photos of ageing stars who try to preserve their good looks. Male or female, seeing someone getting old and still trying desperately hard to be 'sex on legs' is sad. And it's got to be to do with the fact that when somebody defines themselves as the sum of their sexual attrac-tiveness, they do so at the expense of lots of other qualities, like wisdom, or a sense of humour or a philosophical approach – all of which we can acquire with age.

We often hear people say 'I found thirty very difficult' or 'My fortieth was a watershed for me', when talking about their birthdays. When a particular birthday seems especially hard, then it's probably down to the fact that your self-image may be out of kilter with what everyone else is expecting from you. You've got two choices here – you can either say 'What the hell?' to what the world and others think, or decide to go through a period of change.

These opportunities for reassessing ourselves, and how others perceive us, can be very enjoyable, I think. They give us time out to dwell on ourselves for a while. We can use our reassessment to give ourselves treats and new habits that will bolster our self-image. You know, along the lines of 'the thirty-something me does yoga'; 'the 43-year-old me starts to wear top-notch clothes'; or 'in my fifth decade I will drink a glass of fine claret every evening'. When we consciously choose positive changes to support getting older, our confidence is likely to remain high and we will still feel irresistible. Other people are likely to perceive us as 'someone who is kind to themselves' rather than an old crone or washed-out roué.

Handling change

Whatever our age, the extent to which we maintain irresistibility will depend on how comfortable we are handling change. It's really helpful, in today's frantic world, to understand the processes of change in order to make the best of it.

One of the thoughts that can demoralise us as we get older is the feeling that we have lost things. Philosophically, it can be more helpful to regard what's happening as change, rather than loss. So rather than losing our looks – they've changed. Rather than having decreasing energy – our energy levels have changed. There is an inevitability about getting older that is just not worth fighting. It's far better to put our energy into going with the flow and enjoying it as much as possible.

In *Transitions*, William Bridges goes through three stages that are part of all changes. He starts with endings.

Starting with ending

The way we view the ending of anything is often determined by whether the change is forced or otherwise. Let's say you've been told you have to move if you want to keep your job. You'll feel a lot sadder about leaving where you currently live in these circumstances than if you decided to move yourself. It's quite likely that if you've made the decision to move yourself, then you will minimise the impact and significance of your departure. Here's what Katie told me:

> When I decided to leave the large company I worked for and join a very small outfit, I went around telling all my friends that *of course* more would be the same than different in my life. And, indeed, two years on, I still think that at my core

I'm the same person. But being in a very different environment, and having to be much more resourceful and flexible, has changed my self-image for the better, I think. And if I'm honest, I've changed more than I ever imagined.

Very often, we have distinctive patterns in how we end things and make our departures. You may be like me, and decide to leave a social event with the intention of leaving immediately. Or you may be like my partner, who thinks about going for a while, and then meanders around a bit chatting to a few more people, then meanders around a bit more, saying goodbye to everyone and then eventually, about half an hour after the original thought to leave occurred, strolls out. I like my endings clean, decisive, precise; he likes his to be extended, sociable and rambling. Something to do with introversion and extroversion, I bet.

Resolution of endings is important, because it determines how you feel about the present. And when we're presented with change of any description, it's much more tempting to focus our attention on the new and novel aspects of what's happening, rather than to focus on sorting out how we feel about what we're leaving behind. The expectations of others, and of society, may exert pressure here too. Here's Janine, an account manager in advertising:

When I had my first child, all our families and friends were thrilled for us, and expected me to be overjoyed at this new role of mother. But I wasn't. I longed for the company of other managers, for lunches in city restaurants, for my designer suits. I really missed other people – adults – appreciating me, and asking me for my opinions and guidance. I missed feeling that I was part of a thriving business community. I realised just how much I loved my career and that I was in a state of temporary mourning for it.

What made everything worse was that I didn't feel it was right to articulate these feelings to everyone. A lot of women I met through the NCT (National Childbirth Trust) had become what I once heard described as 'born again cows' – hell-bent on breastfeeding until their kids were five, and completely fixated on the role of 'mummy' to the exclusion of everything else. Fortunately, on one of our rare evenings out, I met a new mother with fairly similar feelings to mine. She'd worked in publishing and was desperate to go back to work. We became close confidantes, sharing our taboo longings, and keeping one another sane.

William Bridges also describes the four processes we need to go through to end previous existences effectively:
- **We need to disengage** – This will be from a social group, such as your friends in your old job, or your neighbours in the city. One of the key ideas involved in drug or alcohol rehabilitation is that an addict will need to change their social circle dramatically to avoid bad company.
- **We need to dis-identify** – This involves accepting

that we are no longer who we were and that we may not know who we will be next. So our self-images may feel wobbly for a while. Often, it helps to get an image of who you are – temporarily. Here's Janine again:

> The only way I could cope with the loss of structure and order in my change of role from manager to mum – and the unpredictability and chaos involved in looking after a newborn – was to view myself as a sort of hippychick earth mother, who just went with the flow and hung around cafés and parks. Once I had that image to clutch on to, it seemed much easier to forget the role of manager.

• **We need to experience disenchantment** – During significant change we often feel disenchanted, in that a part of our previous world no longer seems real. And what we judged that previous world to be will be largely determined by what's inside our heads. It's just like the feeling we get when we go back to an old school or college or place we lived and worked. Everything is very familiar, but the spell of being right inside that world has been broken and we feel slightly distanced and detached. Disenchantment may often become disillusionment – when we experience that rueful feeling of 'It wasn't all it was cracked up to be'.

Disenchantment at the end of relationships is very common, especially when our attraction to the other person is based on some sort of archetype we regard them as representing. We may have thought we were shacking up with the perfect wife, or the conquering prince, or the all-caring mummy. When we find out the person is more or less than these roles, we become disenchanted and then dis-illusioned.

• **We feel disorientated** – This is the feeling we experience when we know something fundamental has changed about who we are or what we do, or where we live and work – and it may not be very comfortable. But it's necessary, as our constructs (as mentioned in Chapter Two) readjust to our new situation. This feeling often affects our sense of space and time and/or other senses, like the new mother at four o'clock in the morning feeling that she is in some great timeless dark void of tiredness, or the person who moves to the country, feeling disorientated by the apparent space around him and the silence.

Mooching around the middle

There is a middle stage to any change we are involved in, a kind of limboland, where we feel aimless and disorientated. And the temptation is to act as soon as possible to get out of this vacuum, and to get on with whatever we regard as our next beginning. This is Jesus in the wilderness territory – where we may be apparently inactive, or just going through day-to-day routine in a slightly dreamlike fashion.

This time is very valuable because while we are not superficially performing useful action, our inner life can be vital and constructive. Just like during meditation – in a restful state our brains produce alpha waves, the source of creativity. Our unconscious may be working hard, even though consciously we feel ourselves to be in a state of emptiness or chaos. Writers, like Steven Covey, have discussed the importance of getting comfortable with periods between action and reaction: what he describes as the moment between stimulus and response, which in all sorts of contexts matters as we decide what to do next.

Going into limboland holds symbolic significance for us. We are taking time out to regroup our ideas, sort out our direction and make sense of what is happening to us. Anthony Minghella, for instance, Oscar-award-winning writer and director, went on a retreat to sort out his sense of direction before embarking on his extremely successful screenwriting career.

Where change is making you feel unsettled, you may want to do something similar yourself. Take a break for a few days, or have a day out in a very different environment from the one you are used to. When I lived in London, during periods when my main activity was solitary writing, I would mark the end of projects by walking from South Kensington to Knightsbridge, taking in Joseph, Conran, Harrods, Harvey Nichols and all those other dinky-do shops. While my credit level didn't allow me to satisfy my urges quite as much as I would have liked, I always found these trips energising and revitalising. The last thing I would have wanted was solitude in the peace and calm of the country under those circumstances.

Sometimes, taking a physical journey can help people through limboland – an interesting train ride or a sea cruise, for example.

Instantly irresistible

- Get some momentum into your limboland journey by asking yourself, 'What do I really want?' and 'If I knew for certain I would die in a year, what would I most regret as being unlived?'
- Make absolutely sure you have some time alone.
- You may find it helpful to craft your autobiography and also to keep a diary of your dreams, ideas and insights.
- If people are pressurising you to commit to things and you don't really want to do this, make commitments short-term and with provisos.

Smart starts

Sometimes, your intuition and outside forces tell you it's time to move out of limboland – and it would be great if this could be just an intuitive decision – but in real life this often doesn't happen. In real life, outside needs, such as paying the rent, or a cross partner, often influence when we have to get going again. We have to look for opportunities through research and chatting to people, and then act.

New starts will always need to be fuelled by a sense of: 'This is who I am, an individual who exists, and who has this as their purpose.' Call this ego, or what you like, but it needs to be there. William Bridges comments: 'It is to assert that we are on our own in a much deeper sense than we even imagined when we were originally setting up shop as adults. That process involved only independence; this involves autonomy.'

Instantly irresistible

- Enlist the help and advice of people you trust when you are changing direction. Ask them to what extent they think you are building on what you've done before, and to what extent you might be repeating old, unhelpful patterns. Be direct about your need for their observations.
- Balance clarity about the goals you are seeking to achieve with attention to the process for getting there; that is, what you need to do next and how.
- We often view our lives as linear, moving from one event to another, but this can be limiting. People on courses often find it helpful to draw themselves in the centre of their environment, as they are currently, and then to draw themselves at the start of the change they want to make in their lives, or

having achieved that change. Again, drawing in the environment all around – relationships, dependants, location and leisure-time activities – can be helpful.

- Generally speaking, we underestimate how often people make radical new beginnings. So if you're feeling like it, why not?

Love and irresistibility

When we enter into a relationship with someone else, we agree, albeit without stating this explicitly, to share the story of their life with them. And they, whether they are aware of it or not, come to share our story. In a *Pollyanna* world, these stories would both have comfortable endings of 'And so they lived happily ever after . . .' But, in real life, with almost one in three marriages ending in divorce, 'tis sadly not so.

We often have fantasies about both our own and other people's stories: 'He will become immensely successful, motivated by caring for me and our two children in our idyllic country retreat'; 'she and I will both have successful careers and we will be a thoroughly modern couple sharing everything – demands and profits – equally, and neither of us will want children to upset this balance'; or, 'we will both have good jobs, but looking after our children will be a priority for us both, as will quality of life issues – more important than ambition'.

Life would be much simpler if we could write these stories with assurance. But it's very difficult to know exactly what another person wants and what motivates them, however often you sleep with them. And people change.

When we discover that someone's changed, or that they want something very different from what we thought – and that can happen after thirty years of marriage – we need to ask ourselves whether our two stories can co-exist together and come to some sort of happy ending. Rather than thinking about how we can change the other person's story, it's much wiser to put our energies into thinking how *we* can cope with the changes in their story, or whether we'd be better off in a solo narrative.

The key to staying irresistible to our partners throughout life, I fancy, is in the quality of how we communicate with one another about our stories. That will involve sex, definitely, what sort we want where, when and how often. But somehow, when you see ninety-year-old couples who seem happy together, the aura they give off is not the glow of post-coital satisfaction. Rather, they suggest a contentment reached through years of negotiation and compromise, to reach acceptance and appreciation of each other.

A family affair

So what happens when you are involved in a relationship that you very much want to work, but both of you are also determined to make yourselves professionally irresistible?

I left her because I'd just had enough of playing second fiddle to her career. It was great when we first started living together – loads of disposable income – both of us really into our jobs. But five years on our goals seemed to be very different. She was still obsessive about her work, while I wanted us to concentrate more on our quality of life together. She just wouldn't compromise.

I feel jealous when Richard is doing really well at work and pulling in loads of business. I wish I didn't, but I do. I'd like to be generous enough just to feel sheer joy, but I can't – especially if I'm finding it tough going. 'Course I can't let him see this and I don't know where you draw the line between a healthy competitiveness and destructive jealousy. Ironically, one of the great things we have in common is ambition – but I also fear it may be the quality that drives us apart.

When one of you is a finance director and the other a counsellor, with very different career values, then these problems won't arise. And, as mentioned above, being in a relationship involves all sorts of negotiation and compromise – negotiation and compromise about how dependent we are on one another, emotionally and financially, about where we live, what we eat, who we socialise with, where we go on holiday and myriad other things.

Sometimes, the slight discontent we feel when our other half is soaring may be difficult to analyse. Perhaps they're just much busier and more in demand than we are. Being busy and in demand holds high social kudos, today. Or perhaps they're getting a profound sense of personal achievement from what they're doing, and that irks us because it is something we know we could never get from our current situation.

But, hurray! You guessed it, psychology can help us with this. It's important to be able to acknowledge differences between each of you and what you want. Perhaps you're an extrovert under pressure, through having to make a lot of tough decisions that are detrimental to relationships. Or maybe you're an introvert, finding your sense of task achievement thwarted through the number of people problems that keep hijacking you. Undoubtedly, if you both know what's really important to you, and have some common ground in this, plus an understanding of your differences, you are heading in the right direction – together.

Another idea that can be really helpful is to think of the two of you with your respective careers as being involved in creating a prosperous family business. Viewing yourselves as a unit, you can decide on the minimum the business needs to survive in a week. Then decisions about how to maximise individual job satisfaction can be based on this minimum. You can also use this idea to decide on long-term goals, like property buying or retirement. How will decisions on these matters help your joint business thrive?

Making your joint goals into an entity bigger than, and slightly outside, yourselves, will help objective decision-making – decisions like when to have babies, when's a good time for a sabbatical, dare you risk going self-employed or working part-time. When illness or redundancy strike, then rather than going into a tail-spin based on self-centred responses, plans can be made together to fit the bigger picture.

The key to this idea is that it promotes communication between you. And when we communicate well with someone, we stay involved with them. Relationships die when one person (or sometimes both) detaches themselves from what's going on and just really can't be bothered. When both people communicate well together, they both grow and thrive in the relationship. And that, m'dears, is the key to staying irresistible to each other.

Work and staying irresistible

Mick Jagger and company's efforts notwithstanding, there are some professions where it is much easier to grow old gracefully. Rock stars, footballers, IT and marketing roles, where dynamism and novelty are the essence, do not perhaps allow people to grow old easily. Any place where you can become an *éminence grise*, though – such as politics, business consultancy, journalism, teaching, law and medicine – where accumulated knowledge and experience carries clout, will provide happier pastures to graze out your working life.

So you may need to decide between gambling on a fast fortune in your early years and then mid-career retirement, or a long but less flashy career, where you feel appreciated into old age. How we will do our jobs when we are old is something that never occurs to us when we choose and change careers – our present is too exciting and all-consuming. Indeed, in our world of change and uncertainty, it may be very difficult to imagine that you might be doing the same job when you're a lot older. But somewhere along the way, taking age and appropriateness into consideration would be a good idea – if only to minimise the risk of a mid-life crisis, which is usually to do with not having images of how we will grow old contentedly.

As we get older, too, we need to present ourselves in a modern way and regularly update those most superficial aspects of our presentation – hair, make-up, clothes and accessories. People look irresistible when they suggest 'I care about me' because, as onlookers, we assume this means they would care about us, too. Where this is the overall impression you create, the ravages of time will be less obvious.

This business of keeping an eye on 'what's in the ether' is probably the most important attribute – whether you're employed or self-employed. All of my friends in their sixties, who are still very much enjoying what they do, and who are sought after for it, have this skill. Brian, having had a successful career as a journalist on a national newspaper, thrives as a freelance specialising in the small business/self-employed sector. Tania, having risen to the board of a bank, now advises owners of medium-sized businesses on their investments. Caroline, having been an eminent and much published counsellor, now offers her services for coaching and counselling on the internet. They have all constantly researched trends and markets in their business, and used this knowledge to time their decisions well.

And they have all realised that if there is a need for what you do and you do it well, then even if you start doing it when you are fifty-four and a half, you will prosper.

When we're growing older and wiser, our motivation to work is much more about fulfilment than single-minded ambition. We realise there are times when work should be rightfully insignificant, compared to our relationships, our family and friends. We recognise that all of us are much more than just what we do, and what a person has to offer is way beyond their professional skills.

When we know all these things, we can rightfully feel irresistible contentment.

Goodbye

And so, on that note, and leaving you to ponder a future where you grow old irresistibly and, I hope, disgracefully, I must say goodbye.

I very much hope you've enjoyed this book. My aim has been to educate, enlighten and entertain you, with a subject that I think is fascinating and relevant to so many of us. I hope you've got some useful and inspiring ideas. It's over to you now to go and experiment with these in that wonderful laboratory known as real life.

It's almost certainly a form of avoidance that I like my endings to be clean, decisive, and precise, but there you go. Have fun with this book and be the person you want to be. And as my four-year-old instructs me to sign off his letters: Good luck and happy love.

Recommended reading

Bridges, William, *Transitions* (NB Publishing, 1996)

Bridges, William, *Jobshift* (NB Publishing, 1994)

Cialdini, Robert B., *Influence* (Quill, 1964)

Davies, Philippa, *Your Total Image* (Piatkus, 1990)

Davies, Philippa, *Total Confidence* (Piatkus, 1994)

Goleman, Daniel, *Emotional Intelligence* (Bloomsbury, 1995)

Goleman, Daniel, *Working with Emotional Intelligence* (Bloomsbury, 1998)

Plous, Scott, *The Psychology of Judgement and Decision Making* (McGraw Hill, 1993)

Rowe, Dorothy, *The Successful Self* (Fontana, 1988)

Rowe, Dorothy, *Time On Our Side* (HarperCollins, 1994)

Rowe, Dorothy, *The Real Meaning of Money* (HarperCollins, 1997)

Tannen, Deborah, *You Just Don't Understand* (Virago, 1991)

Tannen, Deborah, *Talking from 9 to 5* (Virago, 1994)

For information on Philippa Davies'
workshops please contact:

www.getupandgrow.co.uk
P.O. Box 54, Penarth CF64 3XF
tel: 02920 705723
fax: 02920 705724